PULLED
A Catalog of
Screen Printing

Published by
Princeton Architectural Press
37 East Seventh Street
New York, New York 10003

For a free catalog of books,
call 1 800 722 6657.
Visit our website at www.papress.com.

Editor: Sara Bader
Designers: Mike Perry & Emily CM Anderson
Photos By: Adam Krause

Special thanks to: Bree Anne Apperley, Nicola
Bednarek Brower, Janet Behning, Megan Carey,
Becca Casbon, Carina Cha, Tom Cho, Penny (Yuen
Pik) Chu, Russell Fernandez, Pete Fitzpatrick,
Jan Haux, Linda Lee, John Myers, Katharine
Myers, Dan Simon, Andrew Stepanian, Jennifer
Thompson, Paul Wagner, Joseph Weston, and Deb
Wood of Princeton Architectural Press
—Kevin C. Lippert, publisher

The text in this book was set with Prestige
Elite, designed by Clayton Smith; and Giorgio
Sans, designed by Christian Schwartz.

Library of Congress Cataloging-in-Publication
Data

Perry, Mike, 1981-
 Pulled : a catalog of screen printing / Mike
Perry.—1st ed.
       p. cm.
 ISBN 978-1-56898-943-3 (alk. paper)
1. Serigraphy, American—20th century. I.
Title. II. Title: Catalog of screen printing.
 NE2237.P47 2011
 769.973—dc22

2010019008

PULLED
A Catalog of Screen Printing

MIKE PERRY

PRINCETON ARCHITECTURAL PRESS, NEW YORK

DEDICATED TO:
MY LATE FATHER, RICK ALLEN PERRY.
THERE ARE NO WORDS.
MY LATE STEP-FATHER, JAMES GENTRY.
AND MY LATE GRANDFATHER,
THOMAS WILLIAMS. YOUR GENIUS
INSPIRED ME. THANKS FOR THE
TACKLE BOX OF PAINT,
WHICH STARTED THIS FIRE!
I HOPE TO BE AS PROLIFIC AS
YOU WERE.

PULLED

TABLE OF CONTENTS

PREFACE
BY MIKE PERRY

THE FIRST TIME I PULLED A SCREEN PRINT WAS IN COLLEGE. AT THAT POINT, I HAD NO IDEA WHAT THE TERM SCREEN PRINTING MEANT OR HOW THE COUNTLESS POSTERS I'D SEEN UP AROUND SCHOOL WERE MADE, BUT I KNEW I WANTED TO LEARN. I SIGNED UP FOR A CLASS AND FELL IN LOVE INSTANTLY. STUDYING GRAPHIC DESIGN, I'D FELT LIKE I WAS

FOREVER DESIGNING MOCK-UPS, AND SUDDENLY, THERE I WAS, MAKING SOMETHING. I REMEMBER, PARTICULARLY, THE FIRST TIME I PRINTED A T-SHIRT. I DESIGNED, PRINTED, AND HEAT-SET THE SHIRT BEFORE WEARING IT OUT THAT NIGHT. PRINTING THAT SHIRT EVOKED THE SAME CHILDLIKE SENSE OF WONDER I'D EXPERIENCED MAKING MY FIRST IRON-ON T-SHIRT, EXCEPT, THIS TIME, I WAS THE SOLE CREATOR.

Despite the advances in digital printing, when I first started screen printing in 2001, it was still cheaper for me to screen print one hundred posters than it was to have them digitally printed. It wasn't just the economy of screen printing that appealed to me but also the culture: the kids who were burning screens in their bathrooms and printing in their bedrooms, and the artists at Space 1026, in Philadelphia, and Fort Thunder, in Providence, inspired me most.

With this book, I hope to share with you my appreciation and love for this work. Every mailing tube and carefully wrapped package of prints I received for this project offered an intimate view of its maker. I could see evidence of the time and energy poured into each print. I could feel the texture, the overprints, the accidents—the labor.

There are things you just can't achieve with digital prints, like the quality of Aesthetic Apparatus's nineteen-color print (pages 26-27). Or Landland's set of proofing prints (pages 122-31) that explores the effect of overlapping images. Or Seripop's equally dense and delightful prints that push layering, overprinting, and abstraction (pages 208-21). There is so much process, care, and craft in this work.

In many ways, I still feel that same sense of wonder, thrill, and nostalgia every time I pull a print, and I'm excited to share that passion. It seems only fitting to produce a book that is not only a survey but also a how-to; it wouldn't be in the spirit of screen printing to do anything less than get your hands dirty. Now that I spend so much time in front of a computer, I savor every chance I get to print. You just can't beat what happens when ink is laid down on paper: it smells good, it's messy, and it takes some muscle. It gets me moving and it moves me. I can only hope it does the same for you.

HOW to SCREEN PRINT

AN ABBREVIATED & LONG-WINDED GUIDE to ONE of the MANY WAYS to TAKE CARE of BUSINESS

by DAN BLACK of LANDLAND

① PREPARE YOUR FILM POSITIVE

→ PHOTOCOPY your ART ONTO A TRANSPARENCY... OR, IF YOU WANT TO DO IT THE REALLY MESSY WAY, COAT A PAPER PHOTOCOPY IN OLIVE OIL TO MAKE IT MORE TRANSLUCENT.

② COAT YOUR SCREEN

→ USE A SCOOP COATER (OR your SQUEEGEE) to APPLY A THIN, EVEN LAYER of EMULSION TO THE BOTTOM (FLAT) SIDE OF YOUR SCREEN.

→ EMULSION is SENSITIVE TO LIGHT, SO KEEP YOUR COATED SCREEN IN THE DARK AS IT DRIES.

③ BURN YOUR SCREEN

THERE ARE *probably* A MILLION WAYS TO DO THIS... HERE'S A SIMPLE ONE:

→ HANG A POWERFUL FLOODLIGHT DIRECTLY ABOVE your PRINTING TABLE.

→ PLACE the SCREEN TOP DOWN ON A THICK PIECE OF SOFT, BLACK FOAM.

→ PLACE YOUR POSITIVE FACE DOWN ON THE SCREEN (IT WILL LOOK BACKWARDS).

→ THEN PLACE A HEAVY PIECE OF NON-UV RESISTANT GLASS ON TOP OF THAT TO PRESS EVERYTHING TIGHTLY TOGETHER. THIS IS IMPORTANT.

→ TURN the LIGHT ON FOR A SET AMOUNT OF TIME. KNOWING HOW LONG IS TRICKY, AND IT DEPENDS ON A WHOLE BUNCH OF THINGS. DO TESTS, BE PATIENT, AND WON'T WORK RIGHT AWAY. KNOW THAT IT PROBABLY THAT'S NORMAL IN THE BEGINNING.

③ BURN YOUR SCREEN (CONTINUED)

→ GET YOUR SCREEN OVER to the SINK (or BATHTUB) AND SPRAY IT WITH WATER UNTIL THE IMAGE APPEARS. MAKE SURE TO GET **ALL** OF THE EMULSION OUT of the PRINT AREA.

→ SET IT UNDER A FAN TO DRY if You WANT TO. WHY NOT?

→ AFTER the SCREEN IS DRY, CHECK IT FOR PINHOLES, WHICH CAN BE FILLED with SMALL DABS of EMULSION, OR LITTLE SQUARES of PACKING TAPE STUCK TO THE BOTTOM of the SCREEN.

LIGHT SOURCE

GLASS + ART + SCREEN + BLACK FOAM

④ MORE TABLE SET-UP

→ COVER the CORNERS of the SCREEN AND ANY OTHER UNCOATED AREAS TO PREVENT INK from SPILLING OUT WHERE YOU DON'T WANT IT.

④ SET UP YOUR TABLE

→ CLAMP the SCREEN INTO THE HINGES ON YOUR TABLE. YOU'LL ALSO WANT TO TAPE SOME KIND of SPACERS ONTO THE OPPOSITE CORNERS OF THE SCREEN TO HOLD THE WHOLE THING SLIGHTLY OFF THE TABLE. THIS is CALLED "OFF-CONTACT" and it HELPS KEEP THE INK FROM PRINTING UNEVENLY.

HINGES!

PULLED

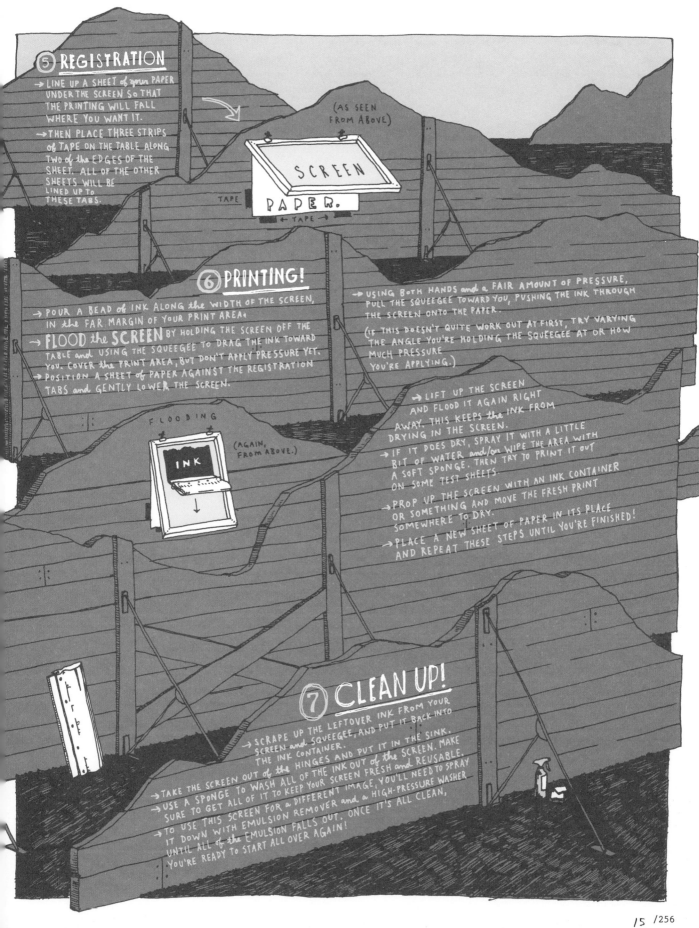

⑤ REGISTRATION

→ LINE UP A SHEET OF your PAPER UNDER THE SCREEN SO THAT THE PRINTING WILL FALL WHERE YOU WANT IT.

→ THEN PLACE THREE STRIPS OF TAPE ON THE TABLE ALONG TWO of the EDGES OF THE SHEET. ALL OF THE OTHER SHEETS WILL BE LINED UP TO THESE TABS.

(AS SEEN FROM ABOVE)

SCREEN

PAPER.

TAPE

← TAPE →

⑥ PRINTING!

→ POUR A BEAD of INK ALONG the WIDTH OF THE SCREEN, IN the FAR MARGIN OF YOUR PRINT AREA.

→ FLOOD the SCREEN BY HOLDING THE SCREEN OFF THE TABLE AND USING THE SQUEEGEE TO DRAG THE INK TOWARD YOU. COVER the PRINT AREA, BUT DON'T APPLY PRESSURE YET.

→ POSITION A SHEET of PAPER AGAINST THE REGISTRATION TABS and GENTLY LOWER THE SCREEN.

→ USING BOTH HANDS and a FAIR AMOUNT OF PRESSURE, PULL THE SQUEEGEE TOWARD YOU, PUSHING THE INK THROUGH THE SCREEN ONTO THE PAPER.

(IF THIS DOESN'T QUITE WORK OUT AT FIRST, TRY VARYING THE ANGLE YOU'RE HOLDING THE SQUEEGEE AT OR HOW MUCH PRESSURE YOU'RE APPLYING.)

FLOODING

INK

(AGAIN, FROM ABOVE.)

→ LIFT UP THE SCREEN AND FLOOD IT AGAIN RIGHT AWAY. THIS KEEPS the INK FROM DRYING IN THE SCREEN.

→ IF IT DOES DRY, SPRAY IT WITH A LITTLE BIT OF WATER and/or WIPE THE AREA WITH A SOFT SPONGE. THEN TRY TO PRINT IT OUT ON SOME TEST SHEETS.

→ PROP UP THE SCREEN WITH AN INK CONTAINER OR SOMETHING AND MOVE THE FRESH PRINT SOMEWHERE TO DRY.

→ PLACE A NEW SHEET OF PAPER IN ITS PLACE AND REPEAT THESE STEPS UNTIL YOU'RE FINISHED!

⑦ CLEAN UP!

→ SCRAPE UP THE LEFTOVER INK FROM YOUR SCREEN and SQUEEGEE, AND PUT IT BACK INTO THE INK CONTAINER.

→ TAKE THE SCREEN OUT OF THE HINGES AND PUT IT IN THE SINK.

→ USE A SPONGE TO WASH ALL OF THE INK OUT OF THE SCREEN. MAKE SURE TO GET ALL OF IT TO KEEP YOUR SCREEN FRESH and REUSABLE.

→ TO USE THIS SCREEN FOR a DIFFERENT IMAGE, YOU'LL NEED TO SPRAY IT DOWN WITH EMULSION REMOVER and a HIGH-PRESSURE WASHER UNTIL ALL of the EMULSION FALLS OUT. ONCE IT'S ALL CLEAN, YOU'RE READY TO START ALL OVER AGAIN!

ENTER

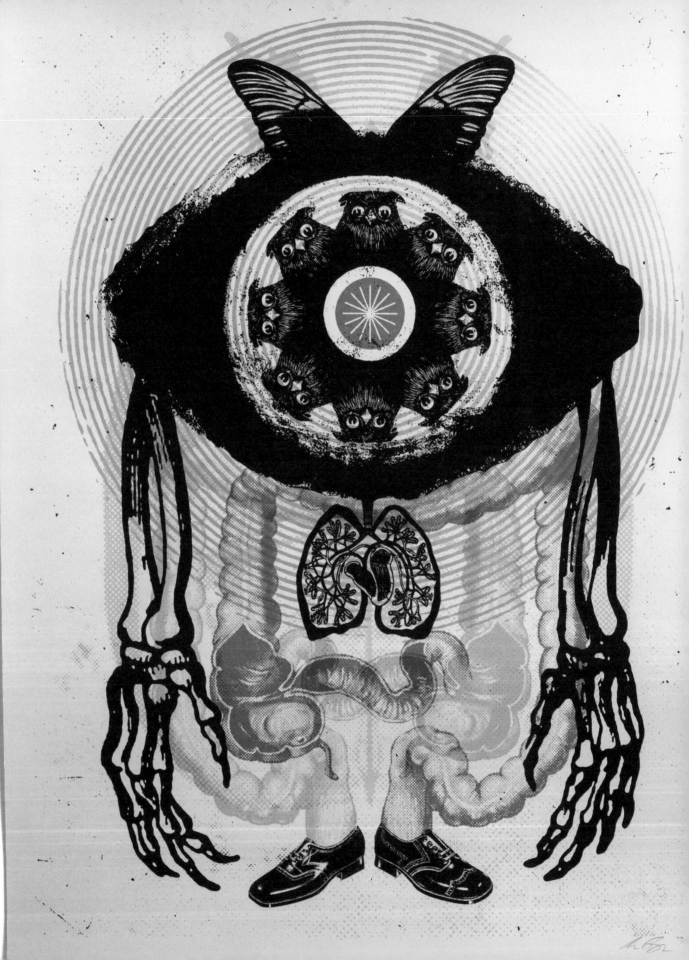

Often considered Minneapolis's best unknown design team, Aesthetic Apparatus was founded around 1999 in Madison, Wisconsin, by Dan Ibarra and Michael Byzewski as a fun side project. Over the years, their limited-edition, screen-printed concert posters have secretly snuck into the hearts and minds of a small, rather silent group of socially awkward music and design nerds. Now, Aesthetic Apparatus is a full-time, full-fledged, insanely unstoppable, and occasionally award-winning design megastudio.

OPPOSITE
Simian Cyclopia, 2008.
Personal.
Art print.
5 color.
Edition of 100.

TOP
Doom in Bloom, 2009.
Doomdrips series.
Art print.
3 color.
Edition of 100.

BOTTOM
Self-Portrait of a Bike Commuter, 2009.
Exhibition,
Artcrank Poster
Show, One on One
Bicycle Studio,
Minneapolis, MN.
Art print.
3 color.
Edition of 160.

LEFT
Nightwindows V3, 2009.
Personal.
Art print.
2 color.
Open edition.

OPPOSITE TOP LEFT
*Doombuddy II:
Mister Tibbets
First Blood*, 2007.
Doomdrips series.
Art print.
3 color.
Edition of 190.

OPPOSITE TOP RIGHT
*Doombuddy I:
Code Name: Mister
Tibbets*, 2007.
Doomdrips series.
Art print.
3 color.
Edition of 190.

OPPOSITE BOTTOM LEFT
*Doombuddy IV:
Mister Tibbets Prince
Of Doom*, 2009.
Doomdrips series.
Art print.
3 color.
Edition of 190.

OPPOSITE BOTTOM RIGHT
*Doombuddy III:
Mister Tibbets
Project X*, 2008.
Doomdrips series.
Art print.
3 color.
Edition of 190.

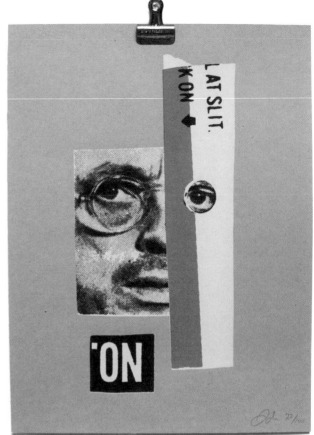

PULLED

OPPOSITE TOP LEFT
Hor Good, 2008.
Frank L. Sprayberry
Presidential
Collage Series.
Art print.
6 color.
Edition of 100.

OPPOSITE TOP RIGHT
Slit, 2008.
Frank L. Sprayberry
Presidential
Collage Series.
Art print.
3 color.
Edition of 100.

OPPOSITE BOTTOM LEFT
Lite, 2008.
Frank L. Sprayberry
Presidential
Collage Series.
Art print.
6 color.
Edition of 100.

OPPOSITE BOTTOM RIGHT
21 Inch, 2008.
Frank L. Sprayberry
Presidential
Collage Series.
Art print.
4 color.
Edition of 100.

ABOVE
Dose, 2008.
Frank L. Sprayberry
Presidential
Collage Series.
Art print.
4 color.
Edition of 100.

PULLED

LEFT
Deal, 2008.
Frank L. Sprayberry
Presidential
Collage Series.
Art print.
5 color.
Edition of 100.

OPPOSITE
*Frank L.
Sprayberry*, 2008.
Frank L. Sprayberry
Presidential
Collage Series.
Art print.
5 color.
Edition of 100.

N YOU FOR

ON

SIVE

FURNITU

G PLAN

NO

Frank L. Sprayberry, President

The Fidelity

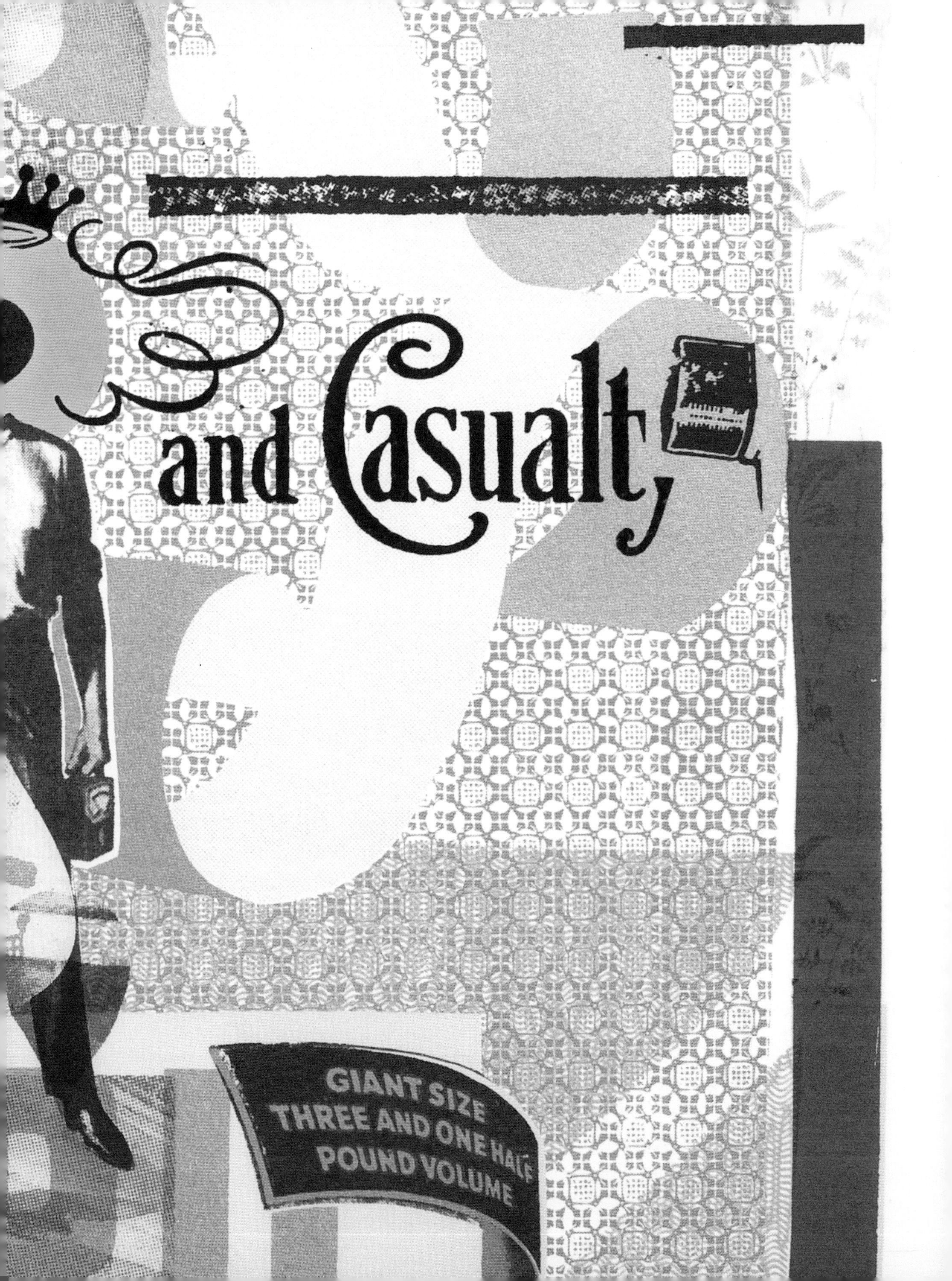

and Casualty

GIANT SIZE
THREE AND ONE HALF
POUND VOLUME

PULLED

PREVIOUS SPREAD
The Fidelity and Casualty, 2007.
Decoder Ring Design
Concern's series.
Art print.
19 color.
Edition of 100.

ABOVE
Test Print #210.
Personal.
Test print.
Colors unknown.
Edition of 1.

OPPOSITE
Test Print #211.
Personal.
Test print.
Colors unknown.
Edition of 1.

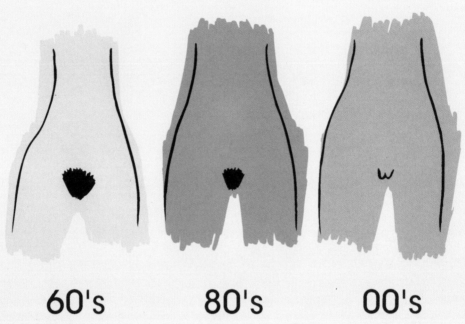

60's   80's   00's

Ashkahn Shahparnia is known for raising the bar and setting new standards in his work. He has been labeled by some as the new bad boy of the art world. Besides smashing the competition and hugging up the haters, he is currently working on mastering the art of cooking brown rice.

OPPOSITE
Evolution of the Muff, 2009.
Personal.
Poster.
4 color.
Edition of 10.

LEFT
I Love LA, 2009.
Personal.
Poster.
2 color.
Edition of 10.

NEXT SPREAD LEFT
Good Vibes, 2009.
Personal.
Poster.
1 color.
Edition of 10.

NEXT SPREAD RIGHT
California Love, 2009.
Personal.
Poster.
1 color.
Edition of 10.

California Love

ASHKAHN

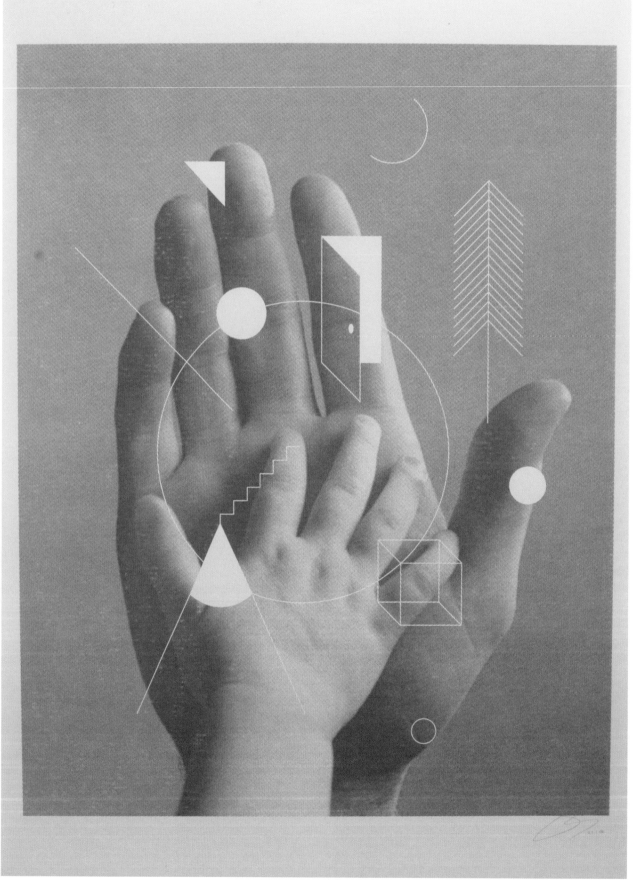

PULLED

Scott Barry is an illustrator and designer
currently attending the masters of fine arts
program at CalArts in Los Angeles. He has
been exhibited internationally and his work
has been featured in various publications,
including *IdN*, *Beautiful/Decay* magazine, and
the limited edition book *So Long Sister Moon*
(Nieves, 2007).

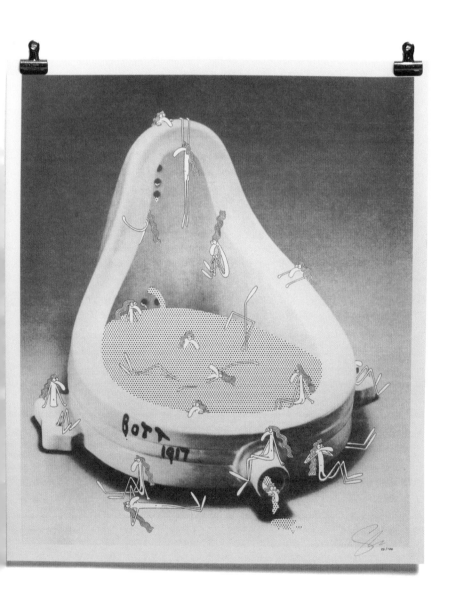

OPPOSITE
Hands of Time, 2008.
Exhibition,
One Foot in the
Other World, The
Other Foot in
the Other World,
Receiver Gallery,
San Francisco, CA.
Poster.
1 color.
Edition of 100.

LEFT
The Fountain, 2009.
Exhibition, A
Small # of Things,
Giant Robot,
San Francisco, CA.
Poster.
2 color.
Edition of 100.

NEXT SPREAD
The Fountain (detail).

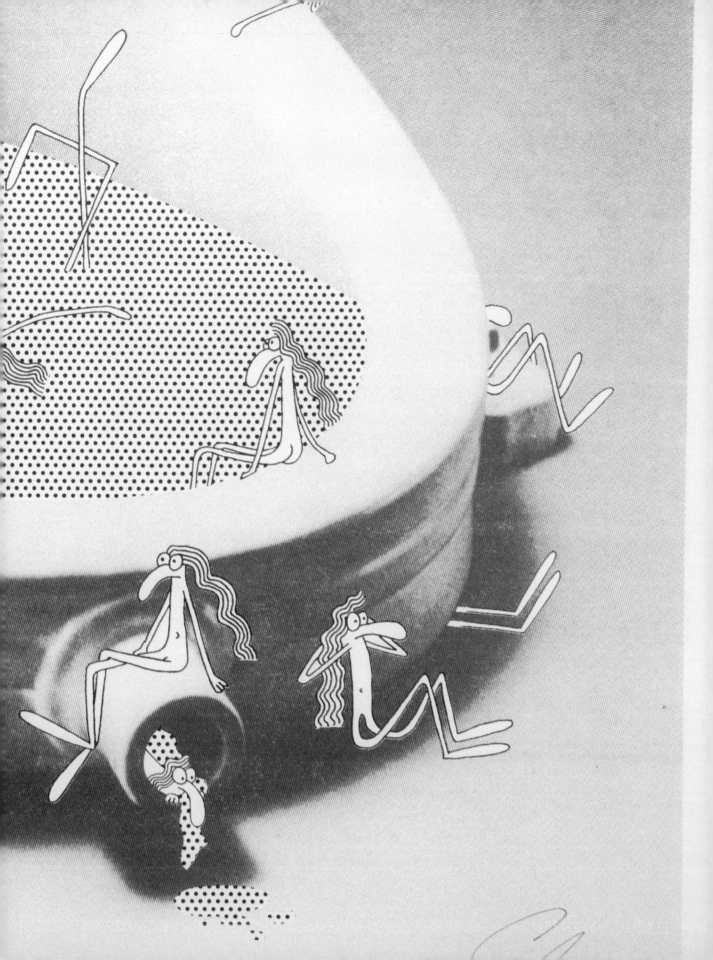

Together / New Mystics

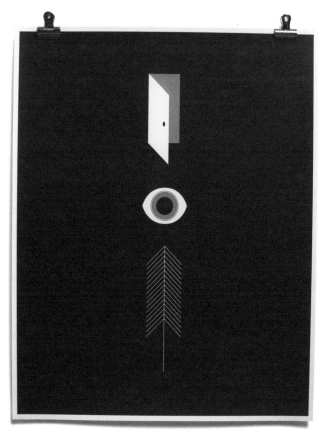

OPPOSITE
New Mystics, 2008.
New Mystics.
Poster.
1 color.
Edition of 50.

TOP LEFT
Haus, 2008.
Exhibition,
One Foot in the
Other World, The
Other Foot in
the Other World,
Receiver Gallery,
San Francisco, CA.
Poster.
3 color.
Edition of 100.

TOP RIGHT
Sight, 2008.
Exhibition,
One Foot in the
Other World, The
Other Foot in
the Other World,
Receiver Gallery,
San Francisco, CA.
Poster.
3 color.
Edition of 100.

Deanne Cheuk is an artist and designer.
She has been commissioned by numerous
companies—including American Express, Dell,
Lane Crawford, Levi's, Nike, Converse,
Sprint, Swatch, Target, MTV, Gap, and Urban
Outfitters—as well as various publications—
including the *Guardian*, *T Magazine* and
the *New York Times Magazine*—for her type,
illustration, and art direction. Her artwork
has been exhibited around the world, most
recently in Beijing, Berlin, Hong Kong, the
Czech Republic, Sydney, and New York City.
Her first book, released in 2005, is called
Mushroom Girls Virus.

OPPOSITE
Untitled, 2008.
Theme magazine
8x08 Print Show,
Art Basel,
Miami Beach, FL.
Art print.
5 color.
Edition of 30.

TOP
Untitled, 2008.
Traveling
exhibition, The
New Grand Tour
Project.
Art print.
3 color.
Edition of 100.

BOTTOM
Untitled, 2008.
Traveling
exhibition, The
New Grand Tour
Project.
Art print.
2 color.
Edition of 100.

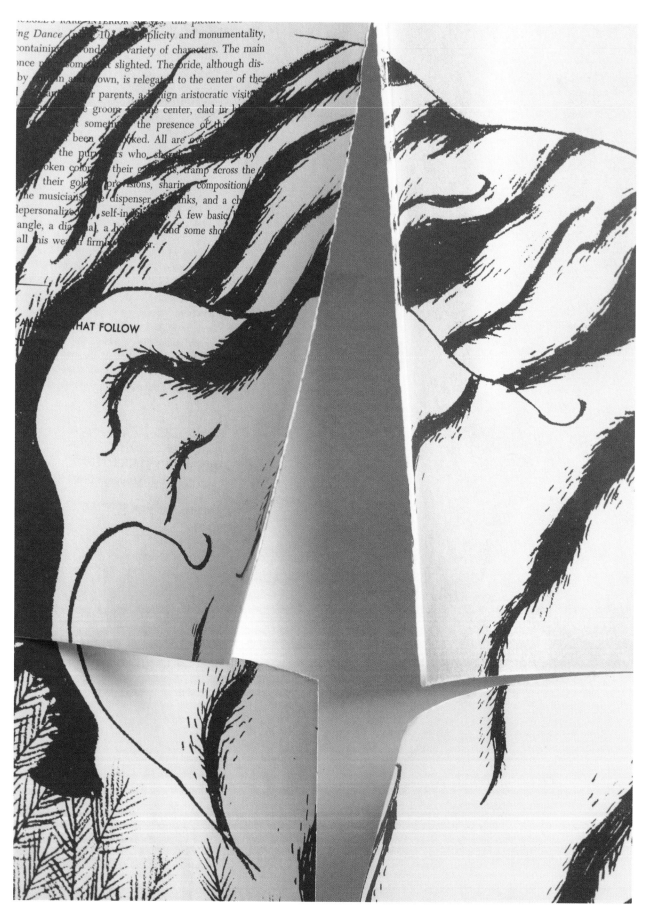

PULLED

Josh Cochran grew up in Taiwan and California
and currently lives in Brooklyn, New York,
with his lovely wife, Jenny, and his small dog,
Porkchop. He graduated from Art Center College
of Design in Pasadena, California, in 2005.
His drawings and prints are commissioned by
a variety of clients in broadcast, publishing,
and advertising. Occasionally, he exhibits his
work in the United States as well as abroad.

OPPOSITE
Inside Path (detail).

ABOVE
Hunters, 2009.
Exhibition, Neon
Monster and Fendi
booth, Art Basel,
Miami Beach, FL.
Art print.
5 color.
Edition of 50.

NEXT SPREAD
Inside Path, 2008.
Personal.
Art print.
2-color silkscreen
with hand-painted
acrylic and gouache.
Edition of 5.

PULLED

Michael Coleman is a graphic designer and printmaker residing in the mid-century modernized hills of Los Angeles' Eastside. He learned print design well before the advent of the Internet and spent his high school years cutting Rubylith films, keylining paste-ups, and bootlegging T-shirts. His studio provides art direction and graphic design for clients such as Girl Skateboard Company, Fourstar Clothing Company, and *Punk Planet* magazine. Recently, Coleman launched Foundation Editions, a curatorial imprint dedicated to the advancement of serigraphy, which publishes and exhibits fine-art silk-screened prints for a roster of international printmakers and artists. His own serigraphs have been exhibited internationally.

OPPOSITE
3rd & Army 03 (detail).

ABOVE
3rd & Army 03, 2008.
Personal.
Serigraph.
5 color.
Edition of 20.

PREVIOUS SPREAD
3630, 2009.
Personal.
Serigraph.
5 color.
Edition of 7.

TOP
Walker 01, 2009.
Personal.
Serigraph.
4 color.
Edition of 10.

BOTTOM
Walker 02, 2008.
Personal.
Serigraph.
4 color.
Edition of 10.

OPPOSITE
Grand Ave. 02, 2009.
Personal.
Serigraph.
5 color.
Edition of 5.

PULLED

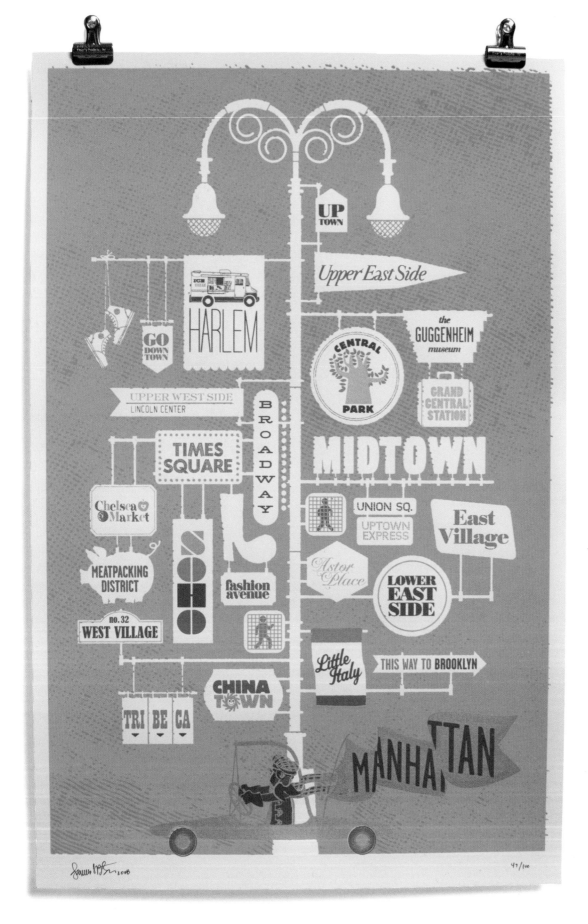

PULLED

Jim Datz is an illustrator, director, and designer who lives and works in Brooklyn, New York. He draws as much as possible and occasionally releases the results into the wild. His small multidisciplinary practice, Neither Fish Nor Fowl, manages a diverse range of projects for clients large and small.

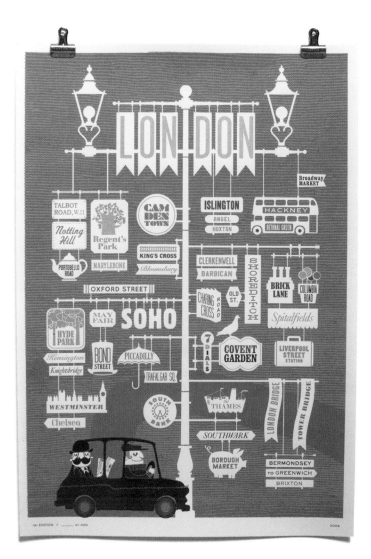

OPPOSITE
Manhattan, 2008.
Three Potato Four.
Poster.
7 color.
Edition of 500.

TOP
Brooklyn, 2009.
Three Potato Four.
Poster.
7 color.
Edition of 200.

BOTTOM
London, 2009.
Pedlars.
Poster.
7 color.
Edition of 400.

PULLED

Justin Fines is an artist and designer
working in Brooklyn, New York. In 1997
Fines founded the graphic design entity
DEMO in his hometown of Detroit. Since then,
DEMO has created work for Adidas, Burton,
Nickelodeon, Zoo York, Nike, Rome SDS, and
many other clients. Fines started regularly
silk-screening when he was a studio partner
at Rad Mountain in Brooklyn. His prints have
been shown in various cities in the United
States, London, and Hong Kong. Most recently
his work was part of a two-man show in
Burlington, Vermont, with Steven Harrington,
and part of an exhibit in Chicago with Chris
Eichenseer, Andy Mueller, and Cody Hudson.

OPPOSITE
Sad Burger, 2009.
Personal.
Poster.
4 color.
Edition of 25.

ABOVE
Poeples, 2008.
Traveling
exhibition,
Off-Register,
LittleBird Gallery,
Los Angeles, CA.
Art print.
4 color.
Edition of 25.

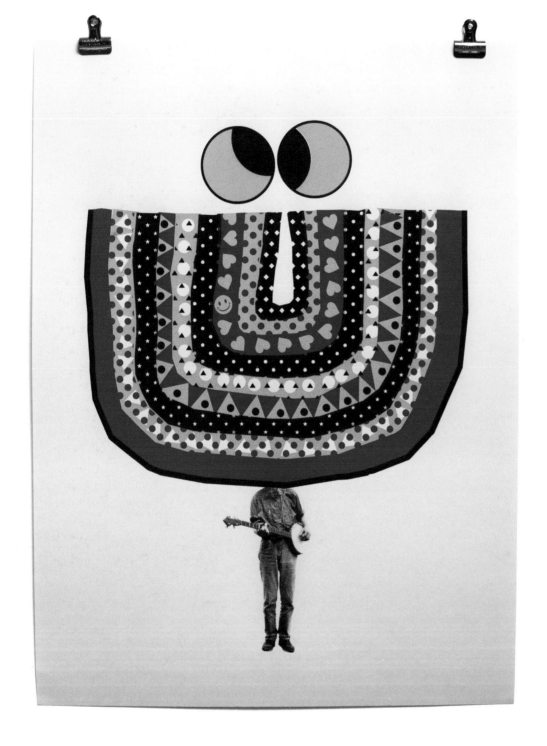

PULLED

ABOVE
Sing!, 2009.
Personal.
Poster.
3 color.
Edition of 30.

OPPOSITE
Junk Drawer, 2009.
Personal.
Poster.
2 color.
Edition of 30.

PULLED

LEFT
Wind-Up Bird, 2009.
Personal.
Poster.
3 color.
Edition of 20.

OPPOSITE
*Upside Down Rainbow
Smile*, 2009.
Personal.
Poster.
2 color.
Edition of 30.

NEXT SPREAD LEFT
*Party Line
(small)*, 2009.
Personal.
Art.
Colors unknown.
Edition of 1.

NEXT SPREAD RIGHT
Homeless Home, 2009.
Personal.
Poster.
2 color.
Edition of 30.

UPSIDE
DOWN
RAINBO
SMILES

PULLED

ALEXANDER ST

PULLED

Rachel Domm makes illustrations, artist books, prints, cards, and more at her studio in Brooklyn, New York. Printmaking has been an essential part of her work since she was first introduced to silk-screening during her school days at Pratt Institute. In addition to art and design projects, she also worked for several years at the artist space and bookstore Printed Matter, as well as for the artist Ryan McGinness, assisting him with his silk-screen paintings and drawings.

OPPOSITE
Forever & Ever, 2009.
Personal.
Art print.
1 color.
Edition of 45.

LEFT
Never Never Never, 2009.
Personal.
Art print.
1 color.
Edition of 30.

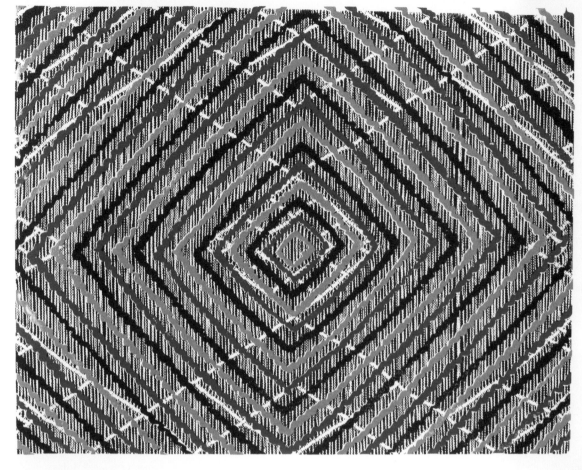

ABOVE
Radiating Diamond, 2009.
Personal.
Art print.
3 color.
Edition of 20.

OPPOSITE
Basket with Basket Pattern, 2009.
Personal.
Art print.
3 color.
Edition of 12.

PULLED

PULLED

E*Rock is a multidisciplinary artist and
electronic musician based in Portland,
Oregon, where he runs the record labels
Audio Dregs and Fryk Beat. His work often
acts as a cultural catalyst. Whether he
is directing music videos, illustrating
for concert posters, DJing, promoting,
producing, painting, printing, drawing,
or running record labels, it's all part
of a larger picture: collaborating with
a greater collective and taking part
in a greater consciousness, with music
as a motivating factor.

OPPOSITE
Wize Wiz (detail).

LEFT
Wize Wiz, 2007.
Bongoût Gallery,
Berlin, Germany.
Art print.
6 color.
Edition of 50.

PULLED

With a studio based in Stockholm, Sweden,
Anna Giertz has been an artist and a freelance
illustrator since she graduated with a masters
of art from Konstfack University College of
Arts, Crafts, and Design, also in Stockholm,
in 2004.

   She has worked as an illustrator and
pattern designer for magazines, books, graphic
profiles,wallpaper, wall painting, fabrics,
and CD covers. Her work has been exhibited
in Stockholm; Portland, Oregon; Las Vegas;
Cologne, Germany; London; and Edinburgh,
Scotland, among other cities. Last spring
she held her first solo exhibition at Galleri
Jonas Kleerup in Stockholm.

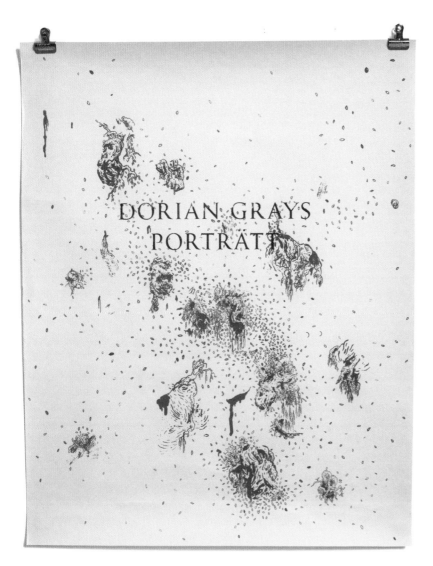

OPPOSITE
Forgetfulness
(detail).

LEFT
*Sibyl, Allan,
Basil, and
James*, 2004.
The Picture of
Dorian Gray series.
Art print.
2 color.
Edition unknown.

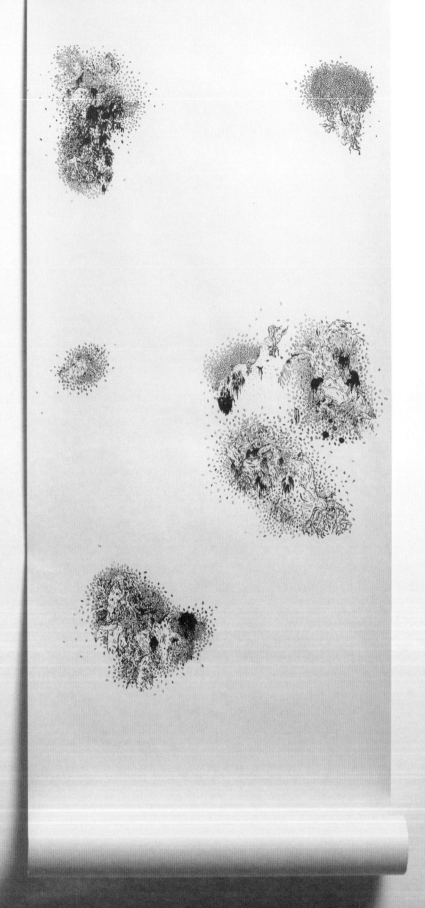

PULLED

TOP LEFT
Opium, 2004.
The Picture of
Dorian Gray series.
Art print.
1 color.
Edition unknown.

TOP RIGHT
Forgetfulness, 2004.
The Picture of
Dorian Gray series.
Art print.
2 color.
Edition unknown.

OPPOSITE
*Behind the
Light*, 2004.
The Picture
of Dorian Gray
series.
Art print.
1 color.
Edition unknown.

GLUEKIT 2009

PULLED

Gluekit is the illustration and design team of Kathleen and Christopher Sleboda. Working from their studio/home in Guilford, Connecticut, Gluekit has been creating illustrations, graphics, and type treatments for clients around the world since 2001. In addition to their commercial work, the pair is passionate about their self-initiated projects, which range from typographic explorations; image and language play; experiments with visual narration and spatial relationships; and illustrations involving baby animals, pop culture, and neon hearts. Gluekit's work has been exhibited in Japan, the United Kingdom, the Netherlands, and the United States. In 2007 the pair established Part of It, a project that works with artists to create products for causes they are passionate about.

OPPOSITE
Untitled, 2009.
Personal.
Art print.
3 color.
Edition of 20.

TOP
Handplant, 2009.
Personal.
Poster.
3 color.
Edition of 10.

BOTTOM
Bricks and Drips, 2009.
Personal.
Poster.
2 color.
Edition of 20.

NEXT SPREAD LEFT
Thunder, 2009.
Personal.
Poster.
3 color.
Edition of 20.

NEXT SPREAD RIGHT
Studio Portrait, 2009.
Personal.
Poster.
2 color.
Edition of 20.

PULLED

id End Street
Mad Cobra featuring the Geto Boys
Columbia 44-74869

First Printing: /25

J. Namdev Hardisty has been bringing
together words and pictures since he was a
teenager making zines on borrowed computer
time. Seventeen years and a bachelor of
fine arts later, he continues that tradition
through books, artwork, and graphic design.
He codirects the creative studio The MVA
with his wife, Kimberlee Whaley. Together
they produce work for Minneapolis College
of Art and Design, Analog Clothing, Corleone
Records, and other clients.

He is the author of two books on graphic
design and visual culture: *DIY Album Art*,
a survey of handmade record packaging from
the 1990s punk and hard-core scene, and *New
Skateboard Graphics*. In addition to making
things, he teaches at Minneapolis College
of Art and Design and runs the occasional
record label, Hardisty-Disk.

OPPOSITE
*Twelves: Dead
End Street*, 2009.
The MVA.
Poster.
1 color.
Edition of 25.

ABOVE
*Listen to
Unwound*, 2009.
The MVA/Hardisty-
Disk.
Postcard.
2 color.
Edition of 50.

Dead End Street
Mad Cobra featuring the Geto Boys
Columbia 44-74869

A1 Dead End Street (Hip Hop Mix)
A2 Dead End Street (Instrumental Mix #1)
A3 Dead End Street (Straight Mix)

B1 Dead End Street (Funky Bass Mix)
B2 Dead End Street (Instrumental Mix #2)

Producer Bobby Digital, Sly Dunbar (A3–B2), Salaam Remi (A1 to A2) — **Co-producer** Tony "CD" Kelly
Engineer Eddison "Elektrik" Sainsbury — **Engineer (Assistant)** Gary "Man" Noble — **Mixed By** John
Pace, Tony "CD" Kelly (A3 to B1) — **Executive Producer** Clifton "Specialist" Dillon

A Midwest Visual Agency product. **www.the-mva.com**

First Printing: /25

edition: ⁶⁸ / **75**

www.m-v-a.com

a public service announcement

keep it thoro

brought to you by midwest visual agency

J. Namdev Hardisty
SMS-C
$20.00

4 of 4

OPPOSITE
*Twelves: Dead
End Street*, 2009.

OPPOSITE
*Twelves: Dead
End Street*, 2009.

ABOVE
*Supreme
Mathematics
Series*, 2008.
The MVA.
Art print.
2 color.
Edition of 75.

PULLED

Steven Harrington lives and works in Los
Angeles. Aside from owning and operating
National Forest Design with fellow artist
Justin Krietemeyer, he still finds time to
work on both commissioned and self-inspired
art projects.

Influenced by images discovered in *Time-
Life Encyclopedia* (1965-1982), thrift
stores, and the music of Bill Withers, his
art might be termed contextual objectivism.
He views each piece he creates as a tangible
object that is part and parcel of a larger
context; the object helps define the context
and the context helps define the object.
Whatever feeling or meaning the observer
takes away from the piece belongs to the
observer. He feels that discovery is the
key. He has exhibited work in Los Angeles,
New York, Dallas, San Francisco, Chicago,
Philadelphia, Montreal, Tokyo, Melbourne,
Barcelona, Paris, Milan, and Berlin.

TOP
Our Mountain
(2 of 3), 2008.
Traveling
exhibition, Our
Mountain, Paris,
Berlin, Barcelona,
and Milan.
Art print.
4 color.
Edition of 100.

OPPOSITE
Our Mountain
(3 of 3), 2008.
Traveling
exhibition, Our
Mountain, Paris,
Berlin, Barcelona,
and Milan.
Art print.
4 color.
Edition of 100.

BOTTOM
Our Mountain
(1 of 3), 2008.
Traveling
exhibition, Our
Mountain, Paris,
Berlin, Barcelona,
and Milan.
Art print.
4 color.
Edition of 100.

Drifter, 2009.
Arkitip magazine.
Art print.
1 color.
Edition of 25.

OPPOSITE
Balance, 2008.
Traveling
exhibition, Our
Mountain, Paris,
Berlin, Barcelona,
and Milan.
Art print.
4 color.
Edition of 100.

PREVIOUS SPREAD
*Past, Present,
Future* (detail).

TOP LEFT
*Past, Present,
Future*, 2008.
Traveling
exhibition, Our
Mountain, Paris,
Berlin, Barcelona,
and Milan.
Art print.
6 color.
Edition of 100.

TOP RIGHT
*Somehow, We All
Seem Connected
Pt. 2*, 2008.
Traveling
exhibition, Our
Mountain, Paris,
Berlin, Barcelona,
and Milan.
Art print.
4 color.
Edition of 100.

OPPOSITE
Smokin' Hot, 2008.
Traveling
exhibition, Our
Mountain, Paris,
Berlin, Barcelona,
and Milan.
Art print.
3 color.
Edition of 100.

PULLED

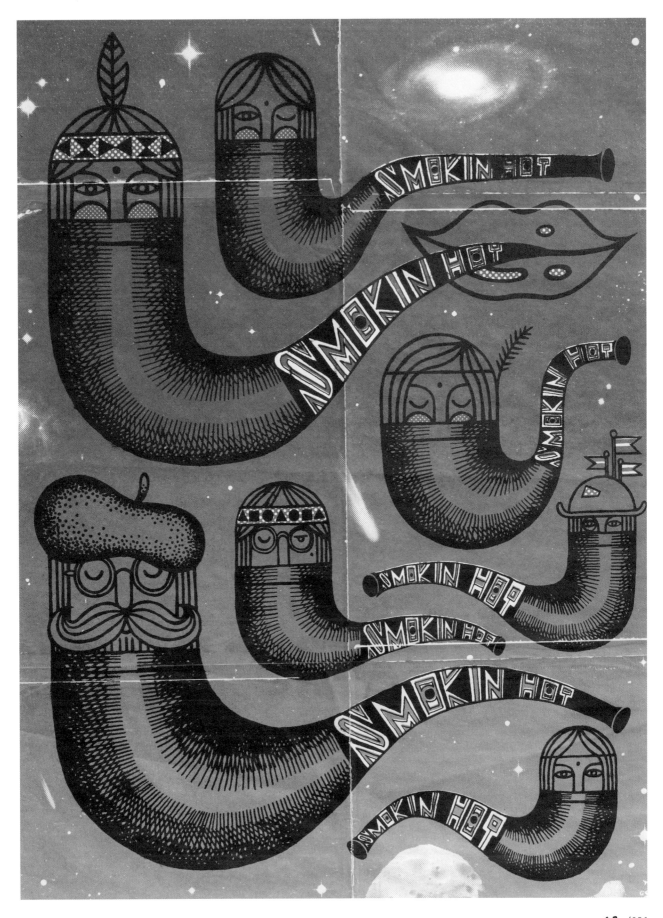

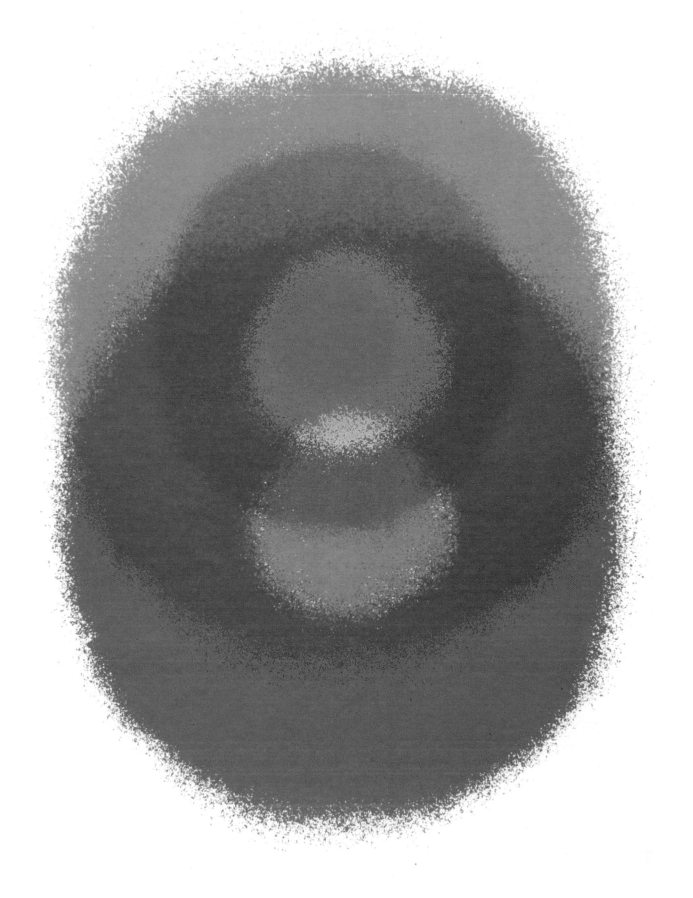

PULLED

Maya Hayuk is a muralist, painter,
photographer, printmaker, musician, and
barnstormer who maintains a studio in
Brooklyn, New York. She has made album
covers, posters, T-shirts, photographs,
video, and stage sets for the Akron Family,
TV on the Radio, and The Beastie Boys,
among others. Her work has been exhibited
and published internationally in galleries,
museums, and in various printed and
electronic media.

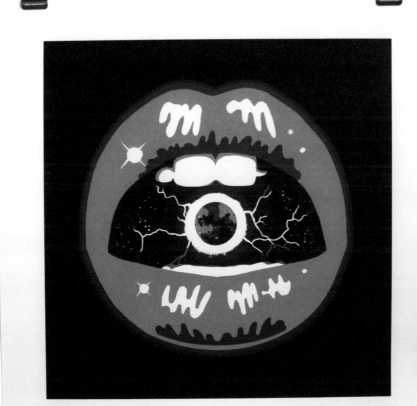

OPPOSITE
*Rings (After Josef
Albers and Chris
Duncan)*, 2008.
Personal.
Art print.
3 color.
Edition of 68.

LEFT
Apocabliss, 2008.
Personal.
Art print.
3 color.
Edition of 25.

TONIGHT IS KINDA SPECIAL   2/45   MAYA HAYUK '09

PULLED

OPPOSITE
*Tonight Is Kinda
Special*, 2009.
Personal.
Art print.
4 color.
Edition of 45.

RIGHT
Guitar Parts, 2008.
Personal.
Art print.
5 color.
Edition of 30.

9z /256 PULLED

Andrew Holder was born in St. Augustine, Florida, and grew up in San Diego, California. He earned a bachelor of fine arts in illustration from Art Center College of Design in Pasadena, California. He continues to live and work in Pasadena, where he illustrates for *National Geographic*, *enRoute* magazine, *GOOD* magazine, and many other clients.

OPPOSITE
Early Bird, 2008.
Exhibition, Neon Frontier, Hibbleton Gallery, Fullerton, CA.
Poster.
5 color.
Edition of 30.

TOP
The Reel Inn, 2009.
Exhibition, Changes, Subtext Gallery, San Diego, CA.
Poster.
5 color.
Edition of 20.

BOTTOM
Vital Organ, 2008.
Exhibition, Neon Frontier, Hibbleton Gallery, Fullerton, CA.
Poster.
5 color.
Edition of 20.

NEXT SPREAD
The Reel Inn (detail).

PULLED

LEFT
Untitled, 2008.
Exhibition,
Neon Frontier,
Hibbleton Gallery,
Fullerton, CA.
Poster.
4 color.
Edition of 10.

OPPOSITE
*City on
Stilts*, 2008.
Exhibition,
Neon Frontier,
Hibbleton Gallery,
Fullerton, CA.
Poster.
4 color.
Edition of 8.

98 /256 PULLED

TOP LEFT
Two Bears, 2007.
Personal.
Poster.
5 color.
Edition of 20.

OPPOSITE
*Two Bears
Revisited*, 2009.
Exhibition,
Changes, Subtext
Gallery,
San Diego, CA.
Poster.
5 color.
Edition of 25.

TOP RIGHT
San Elijo, 2009.
Exhibition,
Changes, Subtext
Gallery,
San Diego, CA.
Poster.
5 color.
Edition of 30.

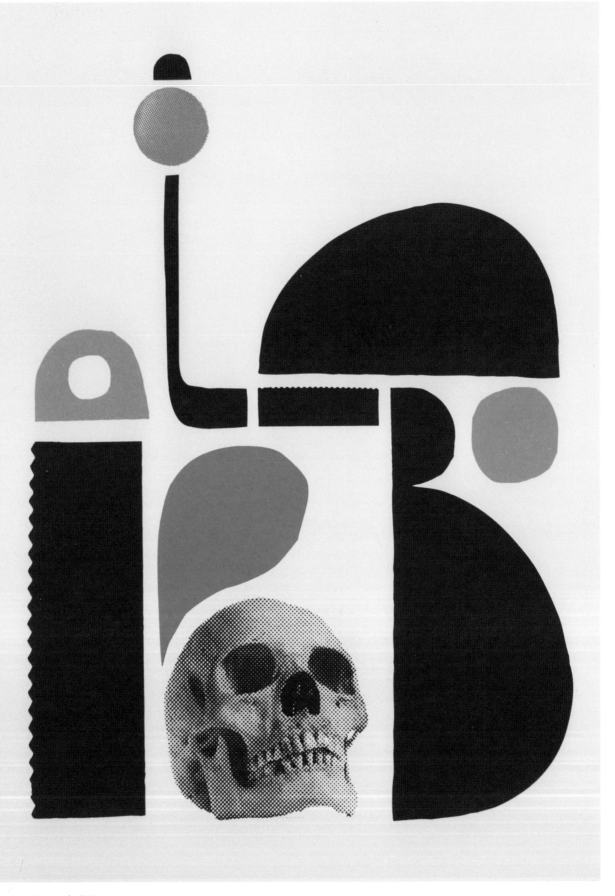

PULLED

Cody Hudson is a Chicago-based artist who is
also the owner and creative director of the
design firm Struggle Inc. His graphic work
and paintings have been exhibited throughout
the United States, Europe, and Japan: the
Museum of Contemporary Art and Andrew Rafacz
Gallery, both in Chicago; New Image Art in
Los Angeles; Rocket Gallery in Tokyo; and
The Lazy Dog Galerie in Paris.

OPPOSITE
Save Skull, 2008.
Personal.
Poster.
3 color.
Edition of 50.

LEFT
*One, Two, Pump
It Up, One, Two*,
2008.
Personal.
Poster.
6 color.
Edition of 50.

NEXT SPREAD
*One, Two, Pump
It Up, One, Two*
(detail).

PULLED

LEFT
One, 2008.
Personal.
Poster.
3 color.
Edition of 50.

OPPOSITE
Two, 2008.
Personal.
Poster.
3 color.
Edition of 50.

NEXT SPREAD LEFT
*Tear The Club
Up*, 2008.
Personal.
Poster.
1 color.
Edition of 50.

NEXT SPREAD RIGHT
Back To Jail, 2008.
Personal.
Poster.
1 color.
Edition of 50.

AP I/III   MONOLITH   Anthony R[...]

108 /256   PULLED

IMEUS DESIGN

www.imeusdesign.co.uk

Anthony Peters, a.k.a. Imeus Design, started his creative career studying fine art on the sunny South Coast of England. After graduating, his love of cubism, fluxus, op, pop, and conceptual art fed into an obsession with graphic design and illustration, especially deceptively simple block color works, screen prints, paper cuts, and pieces containing unusual typography.

Peters currently works as a retoucher, illustrator, and graphic artist. He exhibits regularly in a variety of London galleries and counts the following companies and organizations among his clients, coconspirators, and exhibitors: 2K by Gingham, *GQ* magazine, Airside/It's Pop It's Art, Getty Images, Dalston Print Club, L'Affiche Moderne, the Art Group, *Scarlet* magazine, Manna Records, and the East End Arts Club.

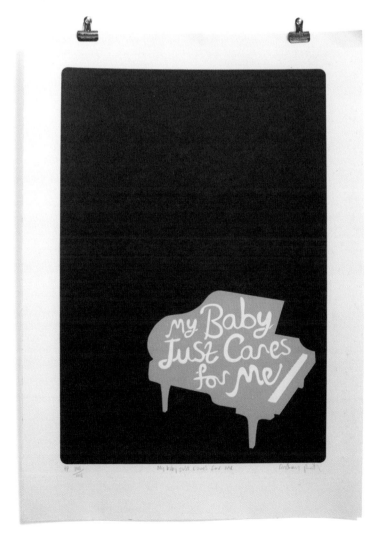

OPPOSITE
Monolith, 2009.
Personal.
Poster.
3 color.
Edition of 20.

TOP
Sea Face, 2009.
Private commission.
Poster.
3 color.
Edition of 20.

BOTTOM
My Baby Just Cares for Me, 2009.
Exhibition, Secret Blisters, Dalston Print Club, London, United Kingdom.
Poster.
2 color.
Edition of 20.

PULLED

Jeremyville grew up in Tamarama, a sleepy beachside suburb of Sydney. He is an artist, product designer, and author. He self-produced his first mass 3-D inflatable designer toy in 1995, and wrote the first book on designer toys, *Vinyl Will Kill*, in 2003. He has been part of group shows at Colette in Paris, the Museo d'Arte Contemporanea Donna Regina in Naples, the 796 Arts District in Beijing, and Giant Robot in New York City. Converse recently released a Jeremyville Chuck Taylor high-top shoe, and *Juxtapoz* magazine profiled Jeremyville in 2009. He splits his time between his New York City and Bondi Beach, Sydney, studios.

OPPOSITE

'Shroom Vibrations, 2007. Exhibition, Kids Today, MTV Gallery, Sydney, Australia. Art print. 3 color. Edition of 100.

TOP

The Streets of Jeremyville, 2009. Solo show, The Streets of Jeremyville, AREA\B Gallery, Milan, Italy. Giant screen print. 2 color. Edition of 200.

BOTTOM

The Breakfast, 2007. Exhibition, Jeremyville NYC, Showroom Gallery, New York, NY. Art print. 3 color. Edition of 100.

NEXT SPREAD

The Streets of Jeremyville (detail).

TOP LEFT
Central Park Jeremyville, 2007.
Jeremyville.
Art print.
3 color.
Edition of 100.

TOP RIGHT
My Summer in Brighton, 2008.
Exhibition, My Summer in Brighton, Castor and Pollux, Brighton, United Kingdom.
Art print.
2 color.
Edition of 20.

BOTTOM
Saturday in Soho, 2007.
Exhibition, Jeremyville NYC, Showroom Gallery, New York, NY.
Art print.
3 color.
Edition of 100.

OPPOSITE
Love in Jeremyville, 2006.
Faesthetic magazine.
Art print.
3 color.
Edition of 100.

PULLED

Kaleidophant is a collaborative project between Therese Vandling and Luke Frost involving illustration, collage, and the exploration of screen-printing techniques. Vandling and Frost are both illustrators, designers, and printmakers. Vandling graduated from the Royal College of Art in London in 2007. Frost is also a member of Heretic, a London studio specializing in screen-printed projects.

OPPOSITE
Unknown Species, 2009.
Kaleidophant.
Poster.
4 color.
Edition of 10.

LEFT
Spacehead, 2009.
Kaleidophant.
Poster.
4 color.
Edition of 10.

NEXT SPREAD LEFT
Parasite, 2009.
Kaleidophant.
Poster.
4 color.
Edition of 10.

NEXT SPREAD RIGHT
Parasite (detail).

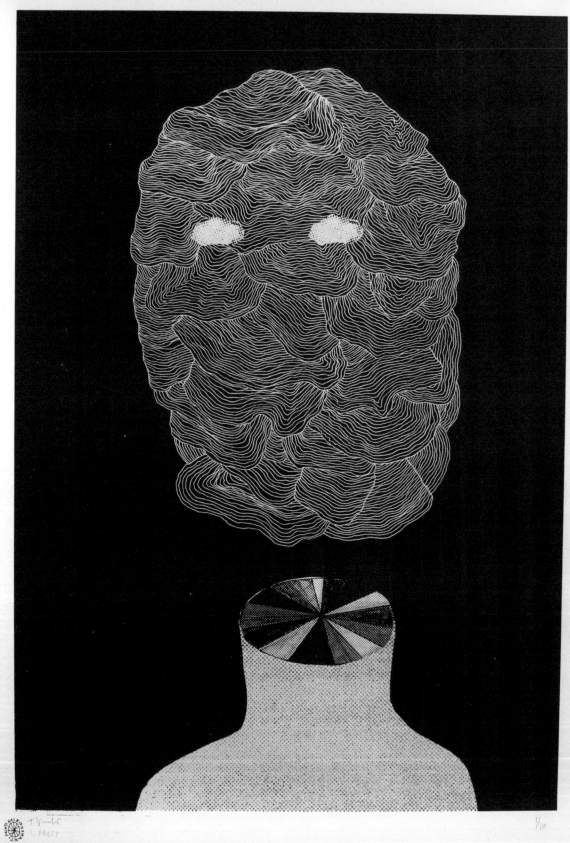

120 /256   PULLED

PULLED

Landland is a very small graphic design
and illustration studio in Minneapolis,
Minnesota, started by Dan Black, Jessica
Seamans, and the late Matt Zaun in the
spring of 2007. The Landland studio doubles
as a fully functional screen-printing
shop, mainly focusing on record sleeves,
posters, and art prints. They will soon
start publishing some short-run books and
a handful of very limited-edition records.
Minneapolis tends to get very cold, so
it often makes sense to stay inside and
draw tessellation patterns or the names
of bands or messed-up billboards or things
that you remember from back when it was
fun to go outside.

OPPOSITE
Untitled, 2009.
Personal.
Test print.
Colors unknown.
Edition of 1.

ABOVE
*A Rainbow Made
of Hair*, 2008.
Personal.
Art print.
9 color.
Edition of 27.

OPPOSITE
Untitled, 2009.
Personal.
Test print.
Colors unknown.
Edition of 1.

ABOVE
Untitled, 2008.
Personal.
Test print.
Colors unknown.
Edition of 1.

NEXT SPREAD
Untitled, 2009.
Personal.
Test print.
Colors unknown.
Edition of 1.

PULLED

LEFT
Untitled, 2009.
Personal.
Test print.
Colors unknown.
Edition of 1.

OPPOSITE
Untitled, 2009.
Personal.
Test print.
Colors unknown.
Edition of 1.

NEXT SPREAD
Untitled, 2008.
Personal.
Test print.
Colors unknown.
Edition of 1.

PULLED

Daniel Luedtke is a self-taught printmaker, artist, and musician from Minneapolis, Minnesota. His brightly colored, bold prints pair geometric abstraction with absurdist, figurative elements that are often inspired by feminist politics, folk art, and kitsch. He got his start by printing posters for his band, Gay Beast, back in 2006 and has since worked on many poster, packaging, and merchandise commissions. After completing a few printmaking residencies in 2008 and 2009, his focus has shifted toward fine-art printmaking and creating larger prints and installations for shows both in the United States and abroad.

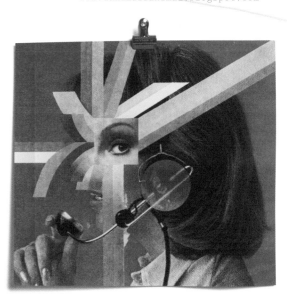

OPPOSITE
Health/Icy Demons, 2008.
First Avenue.
Poster.
5 color.
Edition of 88.

TOP
2nd Wave, 2009.
Personal.
Art print.
4 color.
Edition of 525.

BOTTOM
Banana Wallpaper, 2009.
Highpoint Center for Printmaking.
Wallpaper.
2 color.
Edition of 1100.

LEFT
*U.S. Girls
Variant*, 2008.
Personal.
Test print.
3 color.
Edition of 1.

OPPOSITE
*Figure Study
(Randy)*. 2009.
Created during
artist residency
at AS220,
Providence, RI.
Art print.
4 color.
Edition of 60.

NEXT SPREAD
*Gang Gang
Bananafest*, 2008.
First Avenue.
Poster.
4 color.
Edition of 120.

PULLED

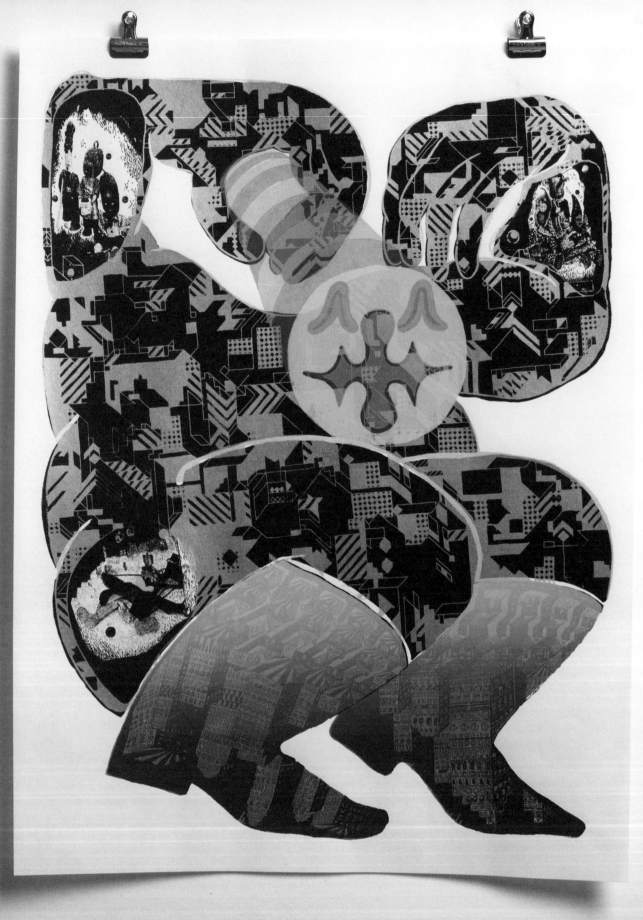

138 /256   PULLED

OPPOSITE
Behold #2, 2009.
Highpoint Center
for Printmaking.
Art print.
4 color.
Edition of 20.

RIGHT
Test #2 (double-
sided print), 2009.
Personal.
Test print.
Colors unknown.
Edition of 1.

DANIEL LUEDTKE

PULLED

LEFT / OPPOSITE
Test #2 (double-sided print), 2009.
Personal.
Test print.
Colors unknown.
Edition of 1.

NEXT SPREAD
Vortex Vacation, 2008.
Exhibition.
Radar Eyes, Co-Prosperity Sphere,
Chicago, IL.
Art print.
4 color.
Edition of 95.

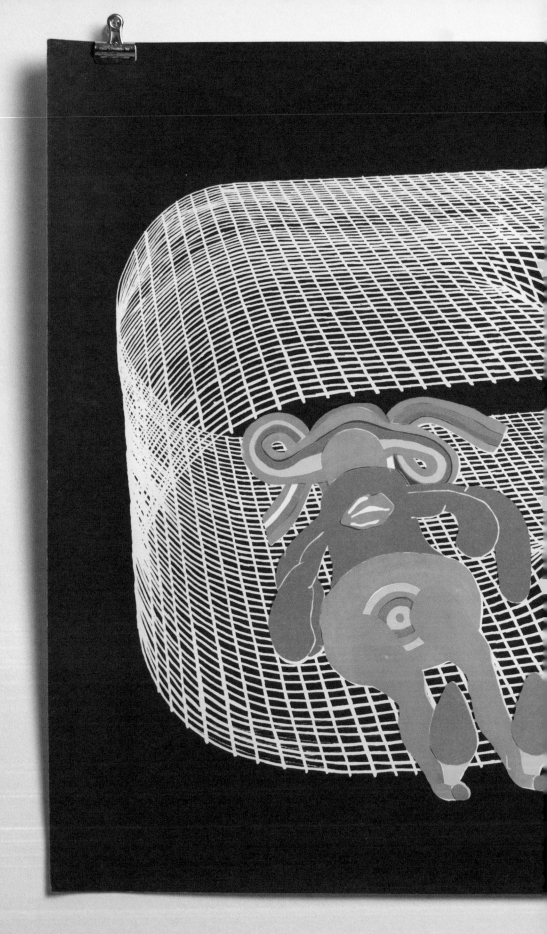

142 /256   PULLED

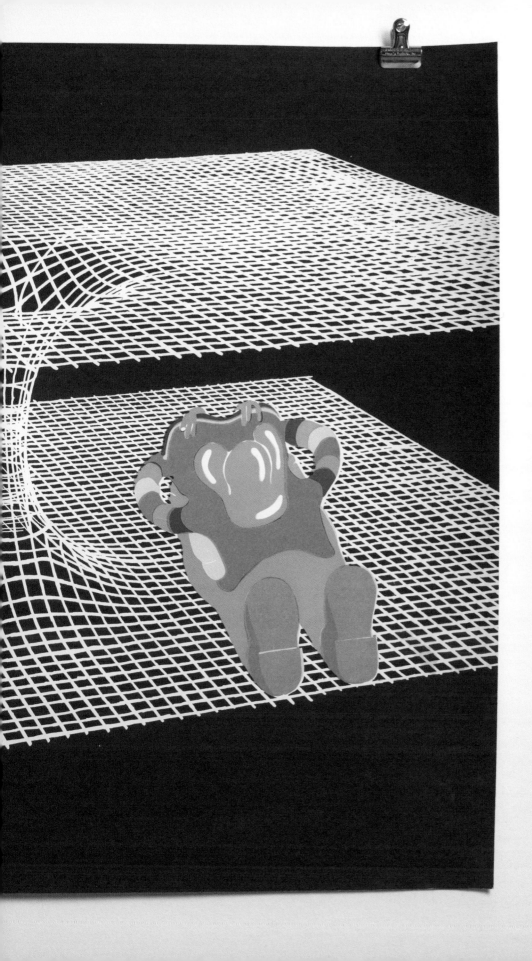

PULLED

DAVID MARON

www.davedavey.com

Residing in Brooklyn, New York, David Maron works freelance as a graphic designer. He graduated from the Cooper Union in 2009 with a background in graphic design, illustration, and printmaking, and thoroughly enjoys making things, including books and prints. Book arts is a passion and personal practice for him, though much of his work is also inspired by printmaking. Maron's professional—as well as personal—interests are in all forms of printed matter, most specifically magazines and art publications. His concern for the livelihood of the magazine industry has heightened his enthusiasm for periodicals. He believes in a constant circulation of creative and original ideas.

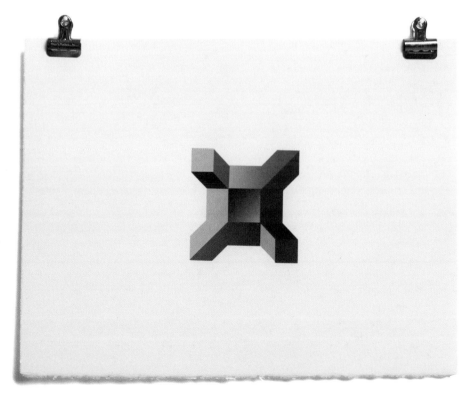

OPPOSITE
Spread the Love, 2009.
Personal.
Poster.
1 color.
Edition of 40.

TOP
Valentine 08, 2008.
Personal.
Poster/gift/card.
2 color.
Edition of 40.

BOTTOM / NEXT SPREAD
A Series of Impossible Occurrences, 2009.
Exhibition,
Whatsoever Things Are True,
The Cooper Union,
New York, NY.
Art series.
3-5 color.
Edition of 90.

PULLED

PULLED

SPREAD
The Earliest Discovered Asteroids, 2009. Personal. Poster series. 2 color. Edition of 30.

pallas

Number 2 Diameter 570 x 525 x 482 km Mass 318,000 10^{15} kg
Rotation 7.811 hrs Orbit 4.61 yrs
Spectral Class U Orbital Eccentricity 0.2299

DAVID MARON

PULLED

Marque is a branding consultancy working collectively across three studios: London, New York City, and Glasgow. The company specializes in position, identity, and communication.

Anna Wolf is a New York City-based photographer from Los Angeles. She has been shooting professionally for almost ten years, working with clients like Quicksilver, American Eagle Outfitters, *Bon Appetit* magazine, and Yves Saint Laurent.

Marque and Anna Wolf came together to collaborate on a series of photo-based screen prints for the New York hotel the Nolitan.

OPPOSITE

Jennifer Marie Sims and Mario Hugo Gonzalez, Artist Management, Hugo and Marie, 2009. The Nolitan. Art print. 4 color. Edition of 8.

TOP

Nina and Julia Werman, Boutique Owners, Valley NYC, 2009. The Nolitan. Art print. 3 color. Edition of 8.

BOTTOM

Keith Phillips, Sales Associate and Visual Merchandiser, Me&Ro, 2009. The Nolitan. Art print. 3 color. Edition of 8.

TOP LEFT
Duncan Quinn and Theodore Crispino, Tailors, Duncan Quinn, 2009.
The Nolitan.
Art print.
4 color.
Edition of 8.

TOP RIGHT
Selima Salaun, Designer, Selima Optique, 2009.
The Nolitan.
Art print.
4 color.
Edition of 8.

OPPOSITE
Nicholas Cox, Chef, La Esquina, 2009.
The Nolitan.
Art print.
4 color.
Edition of 8.

Blake E. Marquis was born in New Hampshire and attended Pratt Institute in Brooklyn, New York. After school he left for Los Angeles to work at Studio Number One, then headed back to Brooklyn to work on various commercial and personal projects. His work has been shown worldwide, featured in numerous publications, and has even picked up advertising awards along the way. In 2010, after exhibiting at Space 1026 in Philadelphia, Blake helped found Mistress, a creative agency. His pastimes include pearl diving and selling short.

OPPOSITE
Unique Vine, 2009.
Personal.
Art print.
24 color.
Edition of 1.

TOP
Unique Vine, 2009.
Personal.
Art print.
23 color.
Edition of 1.

BOTTOM
Hung with Thieves, 2009.
Personal.
Art print.
5 color.
Edition of 1.

156 /256 PULLED

As a designer, bold graphics in black
and white have always been Scott Massey's
favorite to look at and create. Work that
is very raw, experimental, and expressive
is what drew Massey to design and it's
what keeps him satisfied with the career
and hobby. He combines analog and digital
methods when creating designs from type,
graphics, and photos. He finds the more
work done outside of the computer box, the
happier and healthier he is (at this point
he's at 55 percent but he's working on it).
As a designer, he tries to keep all records
of failure in process books and zines. As
an artist, he keeps them out in the open so
he can learn from those missteps.

OPPOSITE
Shed, 2009.
Collaboration with
Paul D'Elia for
RRR.002.
Art print.
3 color.
Edition of 15.

TOP
Wood Pecker, 2009.
Collaboration with
Paul D'Elia for
RRR.002.
Art print.
3 color.
Edition of 15.

BOTTOM
No Life, 2009.
Collaboration with
Paul D'Elia for
RRR.002.
Art print.
3 color.
Edition of 15.

TOP LEFT
Run, 2009.
FND.001 & RRR.002.
Art print.
2 color.
Edition of 15.

TOP RIGHT
*Sikyscreen Combo
(2+4)*, 2009.
Donated to SurfAid
via the Motel
No Tell.
Art print.
2 color.
Edition of 15.

OPPOSITE
*Sikyscreen Combo
(1+9)*, 2009.
Donated to SurfAid
via the Motel
No Tell.
Art print.
2 color.
Edition of 1.

NEXT SPREAD
No Dreams, 2009.
Personal.
Art print.
1 color.
Edition of 15.

pd + fm   Day L   13/14

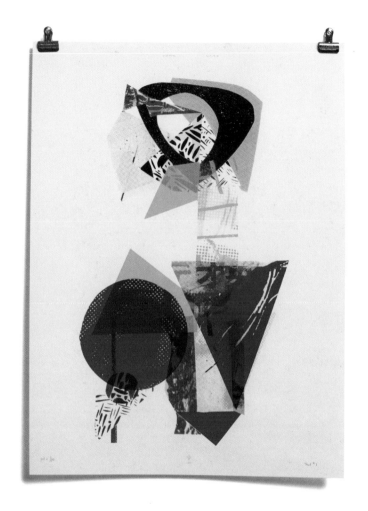

TOP LEFT
Make Ready 2, 2009.
Collaboration with
Paul D'Elia for
RRR.002.
Art print.
5 color.
Edition of 1.

PREVIOUS SPREAD LEFT
Day1, 2009.
Collaboration with
Paul D'Elia for
RRR.002.
Art print.
3 color.
Edition of 14.

TOP RIGHT
Dreamed, 2009.
Collaboration with
Paul D'Elia for
RRR.002.
Art print.
3 color.
Edition of 15.

PREVIOUS SPREAD RIGHT
Make Ready 1, 2009.
Collaboration with
Paul D'Elia for
RRR.002.
Art print.
5 color.
Edition of 1.

OPPOSITE
Division, 2009.
MBR and *MTK* book.
Art print.
1 color.
Edition of 15.

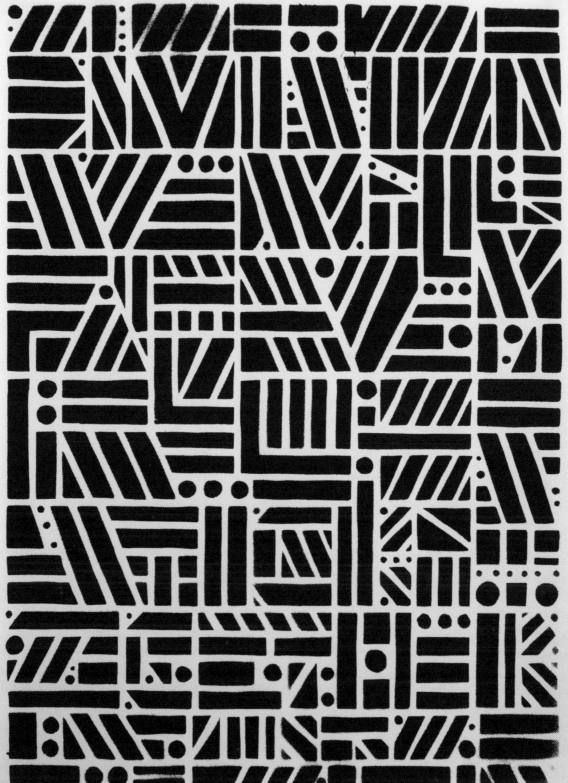

4/15   Division   Scott Massey

PULLED

After graduating from the Rhode Island
School of Design in 2004, Garrett Morin
now lives and works in Brooklyn, New York.
Previously a member of the Rad Mountain
collective, he is now half of Part & Parcel,
a small creative studio that focuses on
design, video, and illustration.

OPPOSITE
Eloie, 2007.
Personal.
Poster.
1 color.
Edition of 75.

TOP
Untitled, 2009.
Experiment.
Poster.
2 color.
Edition of 15.

BOTTOM
Untitled, 2009.
Experiment.
Poster.
2 color.
Edition of 15.

11/12

A MCHR 2009

168 /256   PULLED

Photographer and graphic designer Andy
Mueller was raised in the Midwest on a
healthy diet of BMX, skateboarding, music,
and magazines. Mueller currently works full-
time for the Girl Skateboard Company as the
art director of Lakai Limited Footwear. He
also somehow finds time to freelance under
the name ohiogirl and to run a small T-shirt
line called The Quiet Life. Mueller lives
in Los Angeles with his wife, son, daughter,
two cats, bird, and ping-pong habit.

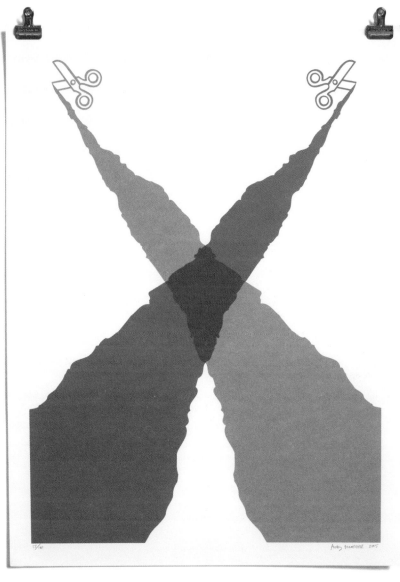

OPPOSITE
Never Stop, 2009.
Exhibition, Public
Works, Andrew
Rafacz Gallery,
Chicago, IL.
Poster.
2 color.
Edition of 12.

LEFT
*criss cross (pink/
green state)*, 2005.
Traveling
exhibition, All
Day All Night.
Poster.
3 color.
Edition of 100.

NEXT SPREAD LEFT
Happy Planet, 2008.
Traveling
exhibition,
Off-Register, AV-
aerie, Chicago, IL.
Poster.
4 color.
Edition of 15.

NEXT SPREAD RIGHT
Sad Planet, 2008.
Traveling
exhibition,
Off-Register, AV-
aerie, Chicago, IL.
Poster.
4 color.
Edition of 15.

4/15

AMUZWER 2008

170 /256 PULLED

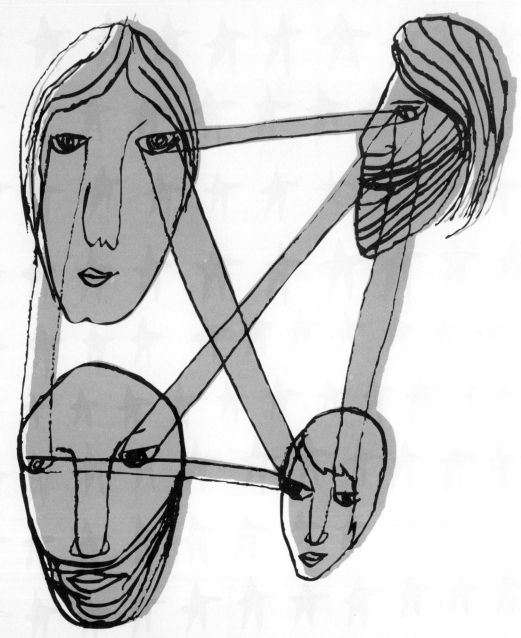

SOCIETY

Andy Mueller 5/100

OPPOSITE
Society, 2007.
Exhibition,
StAAAmering,
The Lab 101,
Culver City, CA.
Poster.
3 color.
Edition of 100.

RIGHT
*Mankind Be
Kind*, 2008.
Personal.
Poster.
2 color.
Edition of 3.

NEXT SPREAD LEFT
*Peace Still
Works*, 2003.
Traveling
exhibition, The
Free Library, M+R
Gallery, London,
United Kingdom.
Poster.
1 color.
Edition of 20.

NEXT SPREAD RIGHT
Love Art, 2005.
Traveling
exhibition, The
Free Library, M+R
Gallery, London,
United Kingdom.
Poster.
1 color.
Edition of 1.

AP

A Mueller 2003

174 /256 PULLED

ANDY MUELLER

Chris Silas Neal is an illustrator and designer born in Texas and raised in Florida and Colorado. His work has been published by a variety of magazines and book publishers and has been recognized by *Communication Arts*, *American Illustration*, the AIGA, the Society of Illustrators, the Society of Publication Designers, the Art Directors Club of Denver, *Print* magazine, and the Society of News Designers. He exhibits drawings at various galleries across the country. He currently works and lives in Brooklyn, New York, and teaches illustration at Pratt Institute.

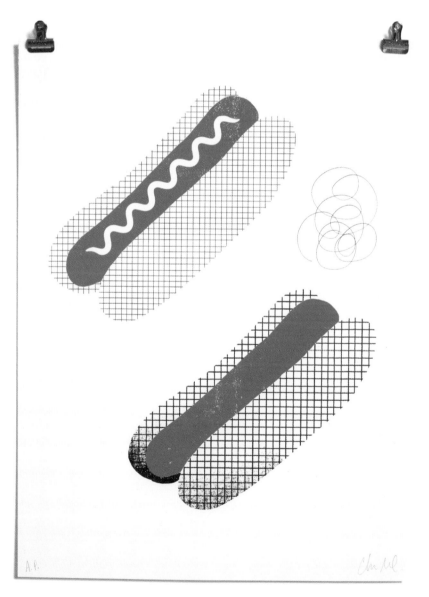

OPPOSITE
Ice Cream, 2009.
Synthetic Foods
series.
Art print.
2 color.
Edition of 20.

LEFT
Hot Dogs, 2009.
Synthetic Foods
series.
Art print.
2 color.
Edition of 4.

NEXT SPREAD
Hot Dogs (detail).

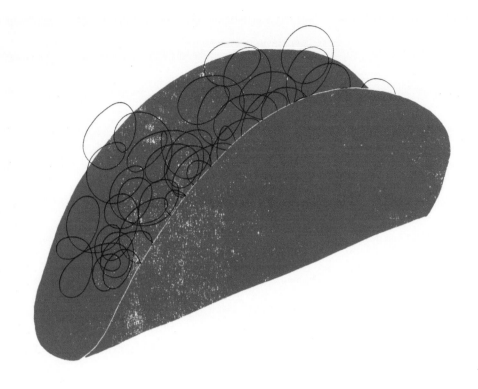

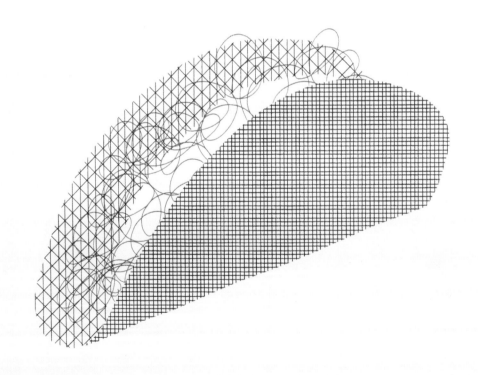

PULLED

A.P.

Chris Neal

OPPOSITE
Tacos, 2009.
Synthetic Foods
series.
Art print.
2 color.
Edition of 20.

ABOVE
Pretzel, 2009.
Synthetic Foods
series.
Art print.
2 color.
Edition of 20.

CHRIS SILAS NEAL

PULLED

Mike Perry works in Brooklyn, New York, making books, magazines, newspapers, clothing, illustrations, drawings, and paintings, and teaches whenever possible. He is the author of *Hand Job* and *Over & Over*, both published by Princeton Architectural Press. He has worked with Apple, the *New York Times Magazine*, Target, Urban Outfitters, eMusic, and Nike. In 2004 *Step* magazine included him in their annual 30 under 30 roundup, and in 2008 he received *Print* magazine's New Visual Artist award and was one of the Art Directors Club Young Guns 6. Perry's work has been exhibited in London, Tokyo, Singapore, Los Angeles, Minneapolis, and New York City. He is also the author of the book you are now reading.

OPPOSITE
Something Inside of Something Else, 2008. Exhibition, Inspired, Tinlark Gallery, Los Angeles, CA. Art print. 3 color. Edition of 30.

TOP
Nine Story, 2009. Exhibition, Giant Zine Art Show, Grass Hut, Portland, OR. Art print. Hand colored. Edition of 1.

BOTTOM
One Step Toward, 2009. Exhibition, Giant Zine Art Show, Grass Hut, Portland, OR. Art print. Hand colored. Edition of 4.

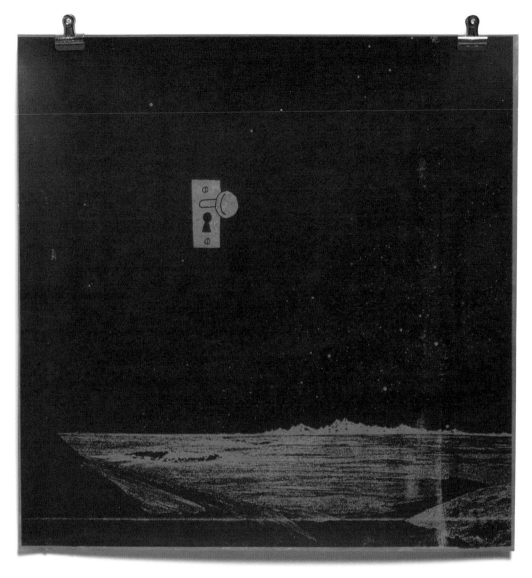

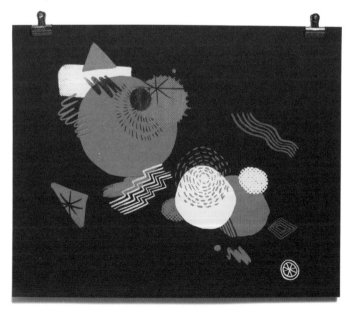

OPPOSITE
*Going to the
Market*, 2009.
Personal.
Art print.
Hand colored.
Edition of 1.

TOP
Door, 2008.
Exhibition,
The Patterns
Found in Space,
Giant Robot,
New York, NY.
Art print.
1 color.
Edition of 10.

BOTTOM
*Love Sour
Love*, 2008.
Exhibition,
The Patterns
Found in Space,
Giant Robot,
New York, NY.
Art print.
4 color.
Edition of 30.

NEXT SPREAD LEFT
*From a
Memory*, 2009.
Exhibition,
Giant Zine Art
Show, Grass Hut,
Portland, OR.
Art print.
1 color.
Edition of 50.

NEXT SPREAD RIGHT
*Hey Over
Here*, 2009.
Exhibition, A
Small # of Things,
Giant Robot,
San Francisco, CA.
Art print.
1 color.
Edition of 50.

PULLED

186 /256   PULLED

MIKE PERRY

PULLED

Finnish illustrator Pietari Posti was
born and grew up in Helsinki, Finland.
After graduating from Lahti Polytechnic
with a bachelor of arts in graphic design,
Posti worked for a few months as a graphic
designer before moving to Barcelona,
Spain, in late 2005, where he pursued his
illustration career. His work has been
featured in numerous publications around
the world, including the *New York Times*,
the *Guardian*, *Wired* magazine, and, in his
own words, "many other magazines no one
has ever heard of."

OPPOSITE
Metropolis (detail).

LEFT
Metropolis, 2008.
Exhibition, Now
Showing: Exploring
the Lost "Art"
of the Film
Poster, Cosh
Gallery, London,
United Kingdom.
Poster.
6 color.
Edition of 100.

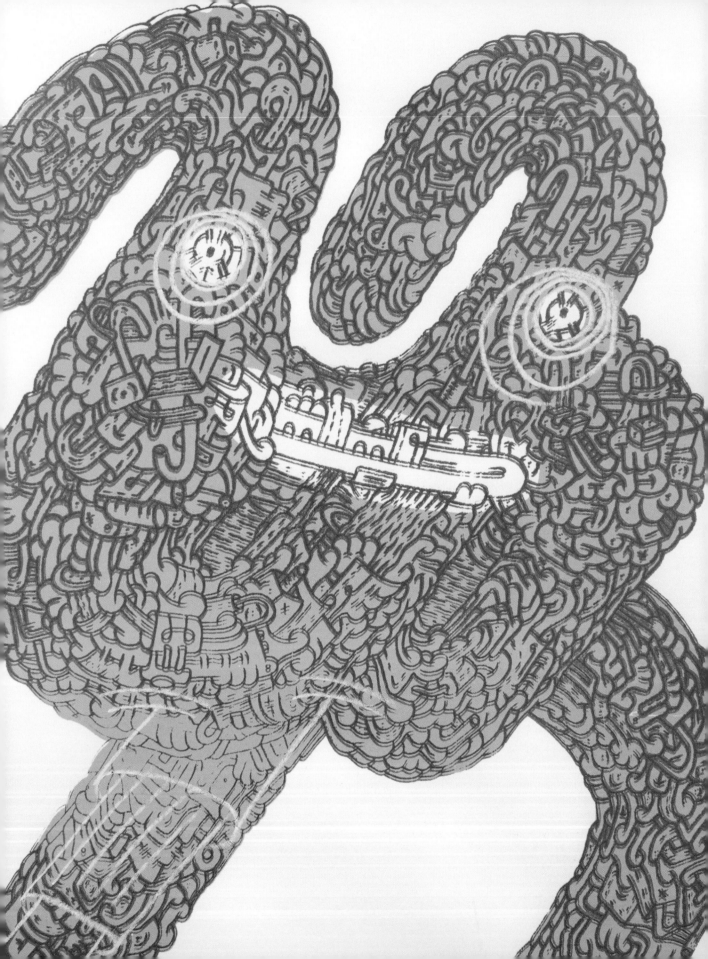

Luke Ramsey is one of the founding members
of Islands Fold, an artist residency located
on Pender Island, British Columbia, Canada.
Ramsey has collaborated with more than
eighty different artists to date and has
exhibited in Bordeaux, Copenhagen, London,
New York City, Philadelphia, Los Angeles;
Portland, Oregon; Vancouver, and Taipei.

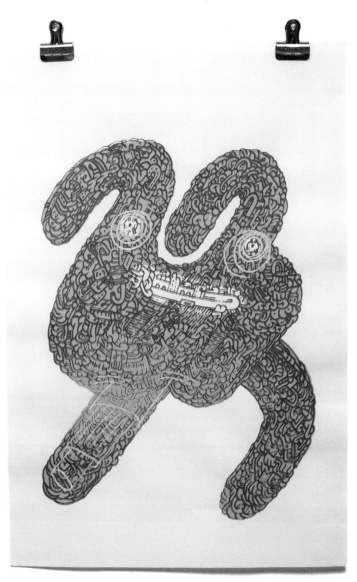

OPPOSITE
Smooch (detail).

LEFT
Smooch, 2004.
Personal.
Poster.
2 color.
Edition of 100.

PULLED

The poster reads: Space 1026 gallery invites everyone to be doodled into a new book by Luke Ramsey's be kind be cause. Opening 8 p.m. Friday April 1st show runs through gallery hours untill book release Friday April 29th 7 p.m. 1026 Arch Street second floor Philadelphia

OPPOSITE

Islands Fold Ethos. 2006.
Personal.
Poster.
2 color.
Edition of 100.

RIGHT

The Be Kind Be Cause, 2005.
Exhibition, The Be Kind Be Cause, Space 1026, Philadelphia, PA.
Poster.
2 color.
Edition of 100.

LUKE RAMSEY

PULLED

Australian design and art collective
Rinzen is best known for the collaborative
approach of its five members, who joined
forces in 2000. Rinzen's work, created both
individually and as a collective, covers
a wide range of styles and techniques, often
featuring utopian alternate realities, bold,
geometric designs, or intricate, hand-drawn
studies. The group's posters and album covers
have been exhibited at the Louvre, and their
large-scale artwork has been installed in
Tokyo's Zero Gate and Copenhagen's Hotel
Fox. Members of Rinzen are spread all over
the world, with bases in Berlin, Brisbane,
Melbourne, and New York City.

OPPOSITE
Slip! Slop! Slap!,
2007 (Craig
Redman/Rinzen).
Exhibition,
Solar Powered,
Kong Gallery,
Mexico City, Mexico.
Poster.
2 color.
Edition of 50.

TOP
On Waking, 2007
(Karl Maier/
Rinzen).
Exhibition,
Solar Powered,
Kong Gallery,
Mexico City, Mexico.
Poster.
1 color.
Edition of 50.

BOTTOM
Happy Ending, 2007
(Adrian Clifford/
Rinzen).
Exhibition,
Solar Powered,
Kong Gallery,
Mexico City, Mexico.
Poster.
1 color.
Edition of 50.

PULLED

LEFT
Stevie, 2008
(Craig Redman/
Rinzen).
Personal.
Poster.
2 color.
Edition of 100.

OPPOSITE
On Reflection, 2007
(Rilla Alexander/
Rinzen).
Exhibition,
Solar Powered,
Kong Gallery,
Mexico City, Mexico.
Poster.
1 color.
Edition of 50.

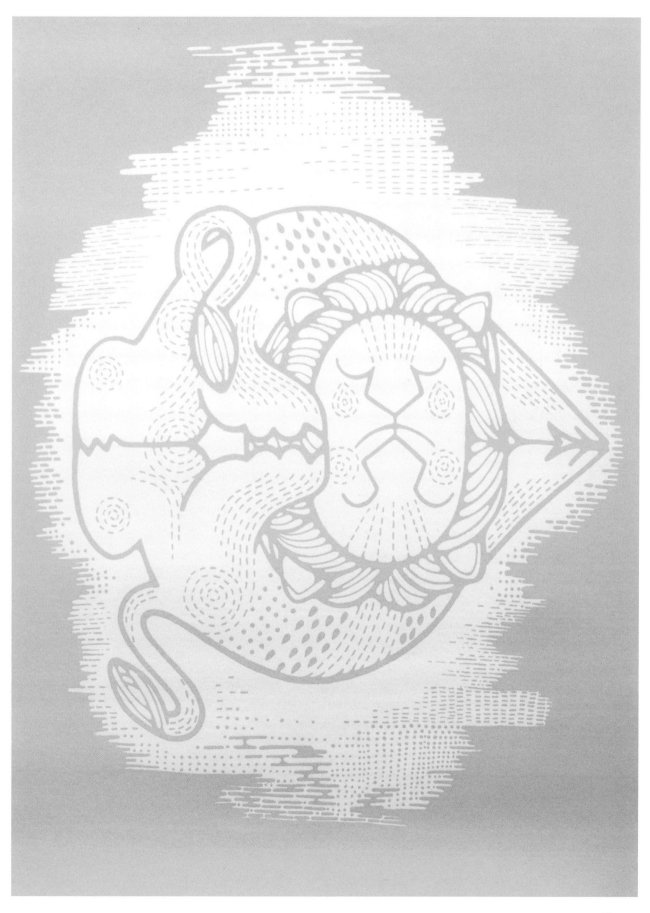

PULLED

Chris Rubino is a New York City-based artist and designer whose work has been exhibited in Europe, Japan, Hong Kong, and the United States. He has created designs and illustrations for such clients as the *New York Times*, Banana Republic, and the Public Theater. He also runs a Brooklyn-based silk-screen studio called Studio18Hundred that makes limited-edition posters for bands such as The Rapture, The Brian Jonestown Massacre, and Vetiver. He is a cofounder of the transitionist art movement. Rubino was chosen as an Art Directors Club Young Guns 5. The Museum of Design Zurich recently added a series of his posters to its permanent collection.

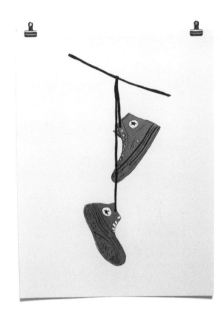

OPPOSITE
Exploding Rainbow, 2009.
Exhibition, Make Believe Maple Leaves, Heist Gallery, New York, NY.
Art print.
Hand colored.
Edition of 10.

TOP
Hanging Chucks, 2008.
Exhibition, The Center of Something, Chashama Gallery, New York, NY.
Art print.
2 color.
Edition of 15.

BOTTOM
Sato, 2009.
Exhibition, Make Believe Maple Leaves, Heist Gallery, New York, NY.
Art print.
Hand colored.
Edition of 1.

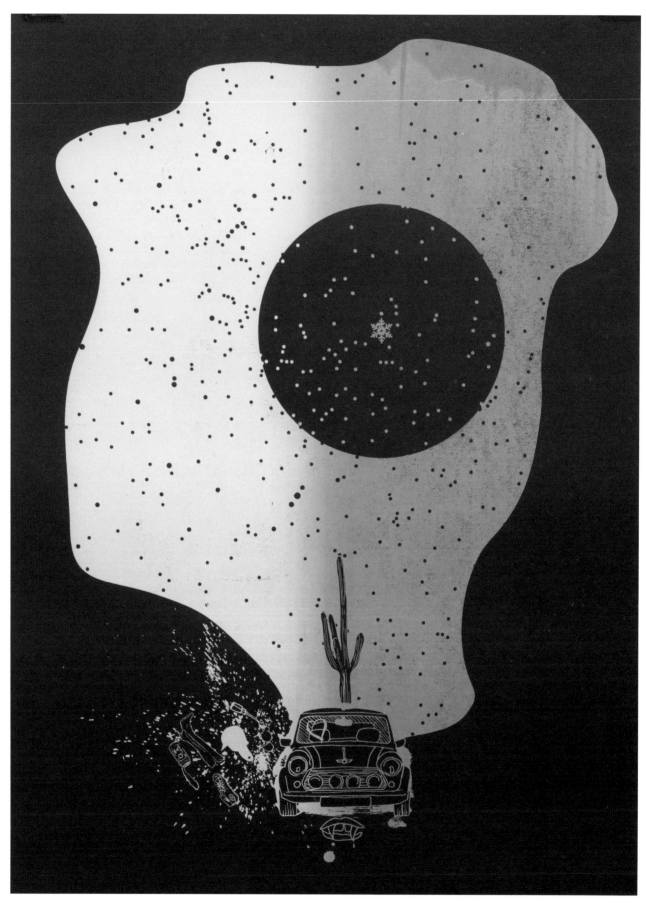

PULLED

FAME & MONEY & STATUS & SUCCESS & SOMETIMES KIDS

OPPOSITE
Joshua Tree, 2008.
Exhibition, Time
Changes, Calm &
Punk Gallery,
Tokyo, Japan.
Art print.
2 color.
Edition of 10.

ABOVE
*& Sometimes
Kids*, 2008.
Exhibition,
The Center
of Something,
Chashama Gallery,
New York, NY.
Art print.
2 color.
Edition of 10.

CHRIS RUBINO

201 /256

202 /256   PULLED

Nathaniel Russell makes drawings, prints, and paintings of mysterious figures, inspirational imagery, new-age posters, primitive characters, dream thoughts, and references to our common subconscious connections. His work has been exhibited in solo, group, and traveling exhibitions in San Francisco, Los Angeles, New York City, London, and Tokyo. Small presses in Scotland, Canada, and Germany have published zines of his drawings. His illustrations have been featured in the Listography series of books, *Dwell* magazine, and on album covers for record labels such as Sub Pop, Bella Union, Secretly Canadian, Asthmatic Kitty, and Brushfire. Russell currently lives and works in Indianapolis, Indiana, after recently moving there from Oakland, California.

OPPOSITE
Open Sesame, 2009.
Personal.
Poster.
1 color (split
fountain).
Edition of 50.

TOP
Blue Tears, 2008.
Exhibition,
New Heaven,
Mollusk Surf Shop,
San Francisco, CA.
Poster.
1 color.
Edition of 50.

BOTTOM
*Petal to the
Metal*, 2008.
Exhibition, Thing,
Big Car Gallery,
Indianapolis, IN.
Poster.
1 color.
Edition of 40.

ETERNAL

& YOU

PULLED

PREVIOUS SPREAD LEFT
*Eternal &
You*, 2009.
Personal.
Poster.
1 color.
Edition of 50.

PREVIOUS SPREAD RIGHT
*Pocahaunted/Sun
Araw West Coast
Tour*, 2009.
Personal.
Poster.
1 color.
Edition of 50.

OPPOSITE
*Personal
Pyramid*, 2007.
Print of the
Month Club.
Poster.
2 color (split
fountain).
Edition of 50.

TOP
Gold Light, 2006.
Print of the
Month Club.
Poster.
2 color.
Edition of 50.

BOTTOM
*Two Days in
Autumn*, 2006.
Music festival.
FolkYEAH!,
Big Sur. CA.
Poster.
2 color.
Edition of 40.

NATHANIEL RUSSELL

PULLED

Formed in 2002, Seripop is the nom de guerre
of the award-winning creative duo Chloe Lum and
Yannick Desranleau. Based in Montreal, Seripop
has earned international recognition for its
stylistically distinct, silk-screened street
posters. In 2005, Seripop began experimenting
with sculptural print installations, which
led to a series of solo exhibitions at Baltic
Centre for Contemporary Art, Gateshead, United
Kingdom; Peacock Visual Arts, Aberdeen,
Scotland; Bongoût Gallery, Berlin, Germany;
and Spedition, Bremen, Germany. In addition to
Seripop, Lum and Desranleau are members of AIDS
Wolf, a noise-rock band, and Hamborghinni!,
a drums and electronics project.

OPPOSITE
Metamorphosis, 2009.
Exhibition, The
Video World Made
Flesh, 107 Shaw
Gallery, Toronto,
Canada.
Art print.
15 color.
Edition of 71.

TOP
Portrait #4, 2009.
Exhibition,
No Henge,
Emporium Gallery,
Montreal, Canada.
Art print.
4 color.
Edition of 80.

BOTTOM
Portrait #2, 2009.
Exhibition,
No Henge,
Emporium Gallery,
Montreal, Canada.
Art print.
4 color.
Edition of 80.

210 /256   PULLED

OPPOSITE
Portrait #3, 2009.
Exhibition,
No Henge,
Emporium Gallery,
Montreal, Canada.
Art print.
4 color.
Edition of 80.

RIGHT
Portrait #1, 2009.
Exhibition,
No Henge,
Emporium Gallery,
Montreal, Canada.
Art print.
4 color.
Edition of 80.

LEFT
Génusss Aux Mitaines, 2008.
Personal.
Art print.
3 color.
Edition of 80.

OPPOSITE
C'est Pas La Prem, 2008.
Personal.
Art print.
5 color.
Edition of 80.

NEXT SPREAD
Untitled, 2009 (detail).
Baltic Centre for Contemporary Art.
Art print.
9 color.
Edition of 80.

PULLED

PULLED

PREVIOUS SPREAD
Mutations
diptych, 2008.
Published by
Twisted Knister
for the Seripop
retrospective
at Spedition,
Bremen, Germany.
Art print.
5 color.
Edition of 25.

LEFT
*Gothik
Thursday,* 2008.
Exhibition,
Radar Eyes, Co-
Prosperity Sphere,
Chicago, IL.
Art print.
3 color.
Edition of 55.

OPPOSITE
Pizza Party, 2009.
Printed on-site
by the artists,
Peacock Visual
Arts, Aberdeen,
Scotland.
Art print.
3 color.
Edition of 70.

PULLED

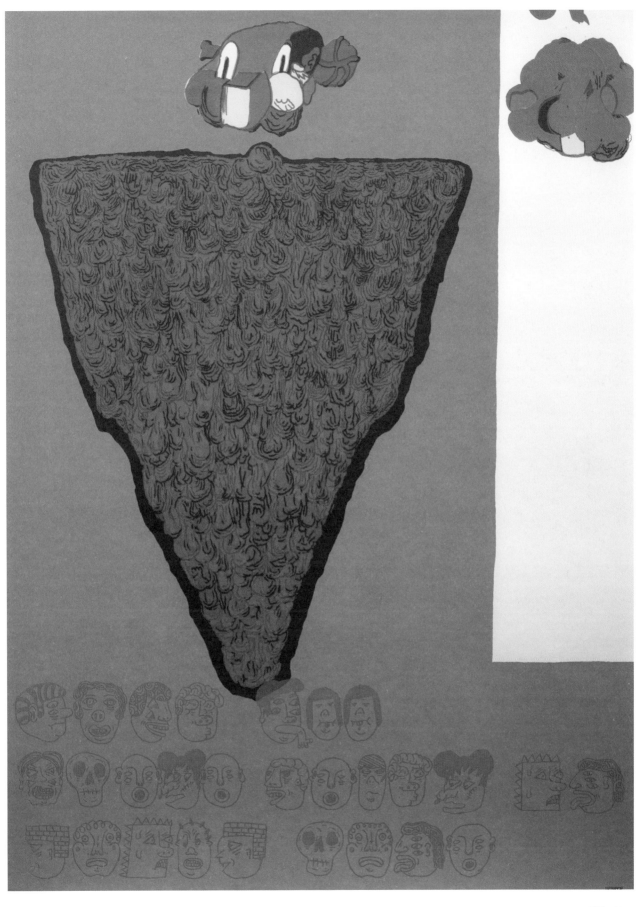

PULLED

TOP LEFT
Sweetly, 2008.
Exhibition,
Radar Eyes, Co-
Prosperity Sphere,
Chicago, IL.
Art print.
4 color.
Edition of 80.

OPPOSITE
*Neatly Pumps
Air*, 2008.
Exhibition,
Radar Eyes, Co-
Prosperity Sphere,
Chicago, IL.
Art print.
4 color.
Edition of 80.

TOP RIGHT
Bummer Road, 2008.
Exhibition,
Radar Eyes, Co-
Prosperity Sphere,
Chicago, IL.
Art print.
4 color.
Edition of 55.

222 /256   PULLED

Andy Smith graduated from the Royal College of Art in London in 1998. He combines illustration and typography to create images that have humor, energy, and optimism. His work has the tactile feel of the handmade and hand-printed despite the fact that it's often created digitally. His client list includes Nike, Orange, Mercedes Benz, Sony, McDonald's, and Expedia. He has exhibited in the United Kingdom, France, the United States, and Australia, and has won D&AD, Association of Illustrators, and Creative Circle awards. He lives and works in Hastings, United Kingdom.

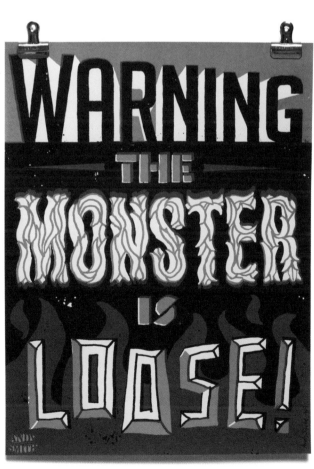

OPPOSITE
Watch This Space, 2008.
Exhibition,
Blisters on My Fingers, Print Club, London, United Kingdom.
Poster.
4 color.
Edition of 35.

TOP
They Went That Way, 2009.
Personal.
Poster.
4 color.
Edition of 40.

MIDDLE
4 Colour Monster, 2008.
Trading card exhibition,
The Monster Mash, Playlounge, London, United Kingdom.
Poster.
4 color.
Edition of 40.

BOTTOM
Warning the Monster Is, Loose, 2007.
Personal.
Poster.
2 color.
Edition of 50.

LEFT
Cinema Français, 2007.
Sight and Sound
magazine.
Poster.
1 color.
Edition of 40.

OPPOSITE
*Relax & Move to
the Country*, 2007.
Exhibition, If You
Could, Exposure
Gallery, London,
United Kingdom.
Poster.
3 color.
Edition of 40.

NEXT SPREAD LEFT
Inergetical, 2009.
Exhibition, The
Art of Lost Words,
text/gallery,
London, United
Kingdom.
Poster.
3 color.
Edition of 10.

NEXT SPREAD RIGHT
Do Not Bend, 2009.
Exhibition,
Blisters on My
Fingers, Print
Club, London,
United Kingdom.
Poster.
2 color.
Edition of 35.

ANDY SMITH

226 /256   PULLED

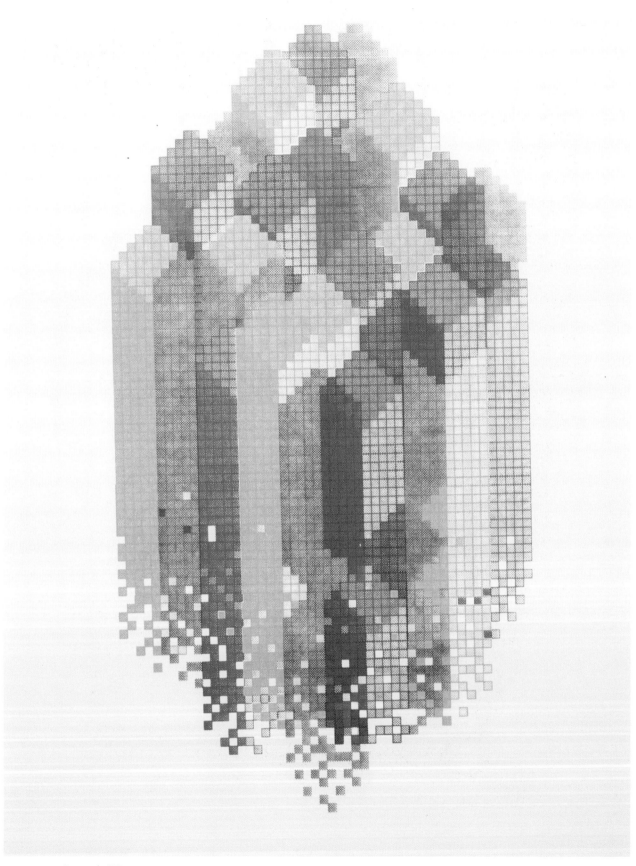

228 /256   PULLED

Marcroy Smith is a graphic designer
and illustrator specializing in screen
printing. He graduated from the University
of Brighton, where he studied under amazing
teachers, including Jasper Goodall and David
Foldvari. After graduation he went on to do
a work placement in New York City with the
creative screen-print duo Urban Inks. Since
then he has managed to scrape together a
living through freelance work for various
publications, bands, and record labels. He
also curates exhibitions and is working
on his side project People of Print, which
is an online directory of print artists from
all over the world.

OPPOSITE
Ceefax, 2009.
Collaboration with
Nic Bennett.
Art print.
2 color.
Edition of 15.

LEFT
*Death of
Protoplasm*, 2009.
Personal.
Poster.
3 color.
Edition of 35.

230 /256 PULLED

Sonnenzimmer is a Chicago-based art and
screen-print studio owned and operated by
Nadine Nakanishi and Nick Butcher. The
couple merges backgrounds in typography,
printmaking, graphic design, and fine art
to create hand-crafted posters, books,
and music packaging for a wide array of
projects and clients. Working closely with
Chicago's bustling free-jazz and improvised-
music community, Sonnenzimmer has found
an environment where experimentation and
abstraction are not only respected, they are
demanded. This freedom has allowed Nakanishi
and Butcher to work through countless
ideas and styles of execution, helping
to shape their visual language, which is
simultaneously quiet and bold.

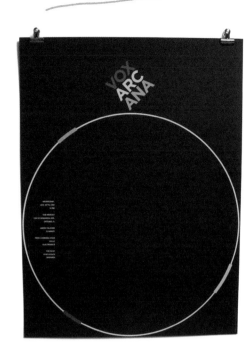

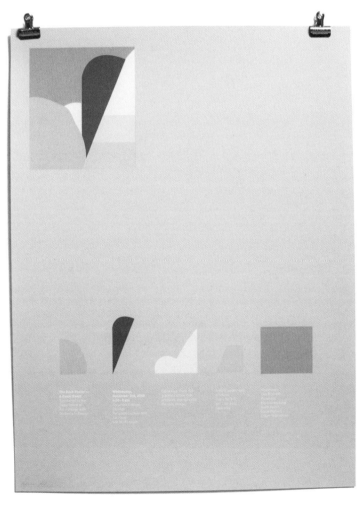

OPPOSITE
*Adventures in
Modern Music*, 2009.
Music festival,
The Empty Bottle,
Chicago, IL.
Poster.
10 color.
Edition of 100.

TOP
Vox Arcana, 2009.
Vox Arcana.
Poster.
4 color.
Edition of 75.

BOTTOM
*The Rock
Poster*, 2008.
Panel event,
Columbia College,
Chicago, IL.
Poster.
5 color.
Edition of 150.

Chicago 2009
Logan Square Auditorium

Saturday, April 25th
with Emeralds

Sunday, April 26th
with Bruce McClure

THROBBING
GRISTLE

PULLED

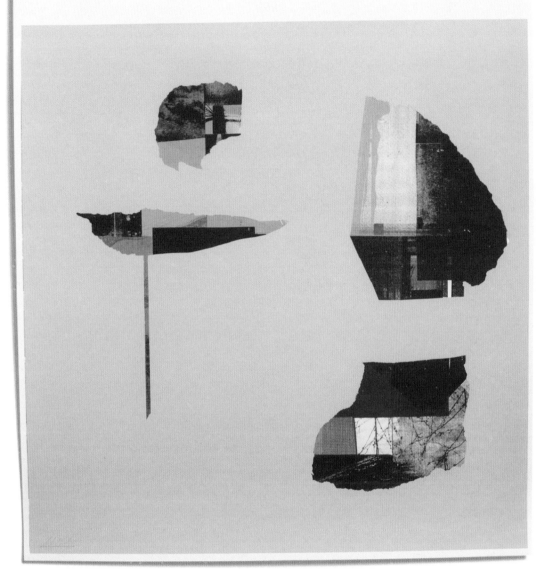

Efterklang
Slaraffenland
with Nick Butcher

Monday, June 2nd
Empty Bottle
Chicago, IL
Free

OPPOSITE
*Throbbing
Gristle*, 2009.
Music festival,
The Empty Bottle,
Chicago, IL.
Poster.
5 color.
Edition of 350.

RIGHT
*Efterklang,
Slaraffenland, and
Nick Butcher*, 2008.
Personal.
Poster.
6 color.
Edition of 50.

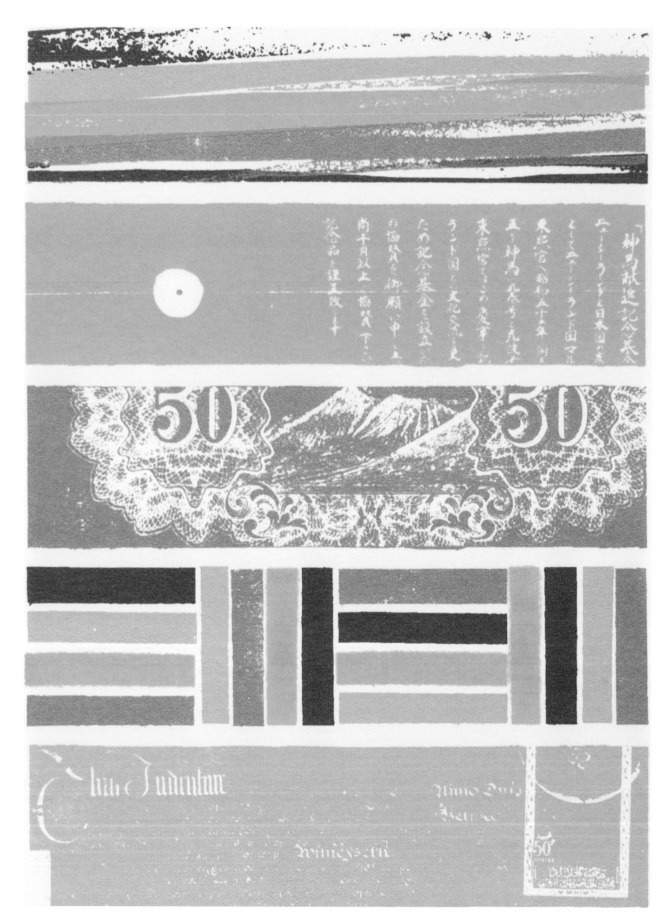

PULLED

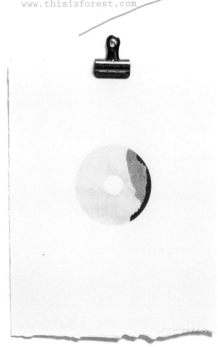

Forest is the multipurpose studio of Joel
Speasmaker, located in Brooklyn, New York,
and covers the areas of graphic design,
art direction, publishing, branding, web
design, illustration, and various curatorial
projects. Speasmaker previously published
The Drama magazine, served as art director
for *Anthem* magazine, and was comics editor
for *Swindle*. He has shown and curated
exhibitions in various galleries, such
as Subliminal Projects, Scion Installation
L.A., DDR Projects, New Image Art, LittleBird,
Lump, Okay Mountain, and Thanky Space.

OPPOSITE
Kyoko, 2007.
Exhibition, Fresh
Prints, Quirk
Gallery, Richmond, VA.
Poster.
4 color.
Edition of 15.

TOP
Surya Narayana
triptych
(1 of 3), 2008.
Traveling
exhibition,
Off-Register,
Foundation
Projects,
Los Angeles, CA.
Poster.
6 color.
Edition of 10.

BOTTOM
Surya Narayana
triptych
(3 of 3), 2008.
Traveling
exhibition,
Off-Register,
Foundation
Projects,
Los Angeles, CA.
Poster.
6 color.
Edition of 10.

PULLED

Jim Stoten lives and works in Suffolk, United Kingdom. He draws as much as he can in lots of different sketchbooks, and occasionally experiments with collage, painting, and Photoshop. He has worked for many clients including Habitat, MTV, Levi's, Urban Outfitters, *The New Yorker*, and the *Guardian*.

OPPOSITE
My Best Friend, 2008.
Personal.
Art print.
1 color.
Edition of 50.

LEFT
Time Drawing, 2009.
Collaboration with Mike Perry.
Poster.
3 color.
Edition of 50.

James Victore is a self-taught, independent artist and designer. Clients include Moët et Chandon, Aveda, Apple, Fuse TV, *Time* magazine, Yohji Yamamoto, Yamaha, and the *New York Times*. Currently, Victore is designing a line of hand-painted surfboards for Design Within Reach, and he recently started the design workshop Sahre Victore Wilker with two friends.

Victore's designs are in the permanent collections of the Palais du Louvre, Paris; the Library of Congress, Washington DC; the Museum of Design Zurich, Switzerland; and the Stedelijk Museum Amsterdam, the Netherlands. He teaches graphic design at the School of Visual Arts in New York City and lives, loves, and works in Brooklyn, New York.

OPPOSITE
Dirty Dishes (detail).

LEFT
Dirty Dishes, 2007.
Dirty Dishes.
Poster.
2 color.
Edition of 300.

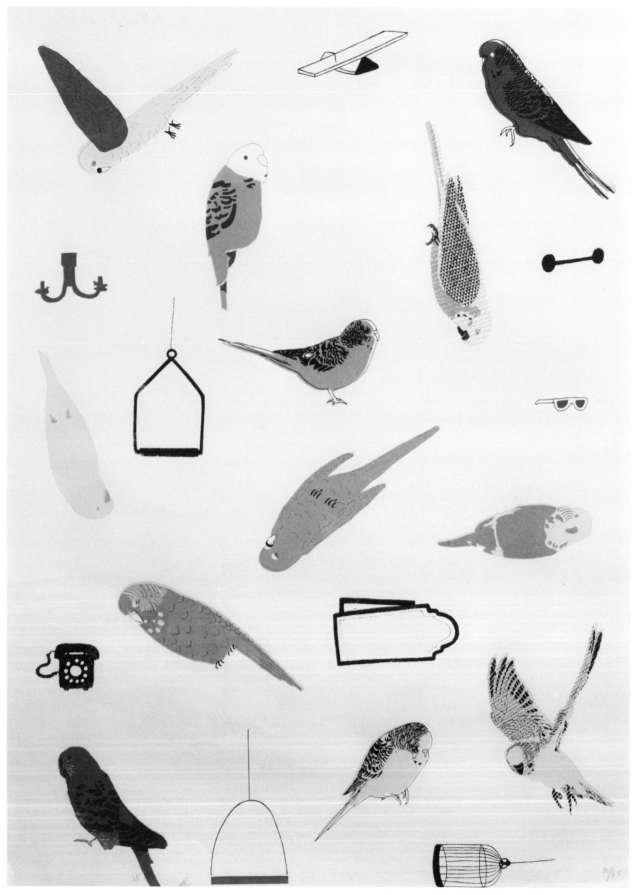

PULLED

Hannah Waldron graduated from the University of Brighton in 2007 with a bachelor of arts in illustration. She has enjoyed working freelance on a variety of projects, while developing her own practice. The issue of reproduction is important to her, and she has been drawn to self-publishing through her interest in screen-printing and bookbinding processes. Waldron exhibits her work on occasion; she uses these opportunities to follow trails of thoughts she feels are worth exploring, in the hope of making connections with subjects she finds fascinating, abstract, or, most commonly, abstruse. Waldron splits her time between London and Berlin.

OPPOSITE
Best Aviary, 2008.
Exhibition, Jayne
Amongst the Birds,
Tatty Devine/Brick
Lane Gallery,
London, United
Kingdom.
Poster.
4 color.
Edition of 65.

LEFT
Best Aviary, 2008.
Exhibition, Jayne
Amongst the Birds,
Tatty Devine/Brick
Lane Gallery,
London, United
Kingdom.
Poster.
2 color.
Edition of 65.

PULLED

SPREAD

*Today I Am a Polar
Bear*, 2008.
Personal.
Poster/book.
2 color.
Edition of 150.

HANNAH WALDRON

PULLED

PREVIOUS SPREAD
*All Animals
Landscape* (detail).

LEFT
*All Animals
Landscape*, 2007.
Personal.
Art print.
6 color.
Edition of 50.

OPPOSITE
*Counterpart
Magazine
ISSUE 2*, 2008.
Counterpart
magazine.
Fold-up poster.
1 color.
Edition of 500.

PULLED

INDEX

PULLED